Tɔ

ل'ٱ

What am I?
And Why Do I Suffer?

An Anatomy of the Human Condition:
Models of Man and Suffering

Iqubal Birdi

authorHOUSE®

AuthorHouse™ UK Ltd.
1663 Liberty Drive
Bloomington, IN 47403 USA
www.authorhouse.co.uk
Phone: 0800.197.4150

Published by AuthorHouse 11/20/2013

ISBN: 978-1-4918-8092-0 (sc)
ISBN: 978-1-4918-8074-6 (hc)
ISBN: 978-1-4918-8093-7 (e)

What am I?
And Why Do I Suffer?

Contents

For my son, Nathan, my wife, Sheila, my family, and
my late father, Surjit Singh Birdi (1935-1972)

Preface

A broad range of academic disciplines—including physics, biology, neuropsychology, neuroscience, psychology, social sciences, cultural studies, anthropology, philosophy, as well as the arts, literature, religion, and spirituality—all continue to contribute to and inform our understanding of human nature, experience, behaviour, existence, and reality.

These bodies of knowledge can collectively offer us increasing insight into the human condition: what it is to be human and the experience of being human, of being in the world, and of consciousness. We can also gain insight into human meaning; how we react to, and cope, with inevitable life events common to all humans i.e. suffering; how we think, feel and act; the person and identity; human mental illness and emotional and psychological distress.

However, whilst useful, the vast array of these knowledge and belief systems, as well as the theories or approaches within them, are often philosophically disparate, heterogeneous, and conflicting in their underlying assumptions, beliefs, and conceptions of the world, reality, and human nature. This may leave the lay person who needs emotional, psychological, and existential help, or awareness and understanding, bewildered and confused, not to mention the frontline practitioners and professionals designated with doing the helping!

This book aims, therefore, to outline, compare, and evaluate—as well as integrate where possible—a broad range of approaches and theories toward holistically understanding human nature, experience, and behaviour and relating these to the human condition, emotional and psychological suffering, existence, and reality.

The author feels these theories and approaches may be seen to be addressing different levels, components, or dimensions of the person, individual, or organism, (i.e. physical, biological, neurological, evolutionary, psychological, sociocultural, and spiritual). Therefore, the book addresses them separately as what he calls 'worlds'—the 'Physical World', the 'Innate World', the 'God World', the 'Social World', and the 'Real World'.

A schematic features at the end of the book (Appendix A), depicting content and concepts from the book as well as the author's representation of the human condition and its levels, components, and processes. These can be used to refer to, or underpin, understanding and for readers' further discussion, exploration, and research.

This book accomplishes the following:

(i)   charts a range of cross-disciplinary approaches and theories relating to human nature, experience, and behaviour, suggesting within each of these how they may be seen to relate to the human condition, human suffering, and to reducing suffering, emotional, and psychological distress;

(ii)   discusses current postmodernist/post-structuralist concerns about the essence of what we are (i.e. whether we really are essential and substantial individuals/persons, or whether we are merely socio-linguistic-cultural constructs or subjects);

(iii) incorporates eastern philosophies and psychologies in relation to what we are in reality, the mind, the self, and human suffering; and

(iv)   identifies, in its conclusion, a number of elicited principles a person may incorporate into their daily living to reduce their suffering and increase their psychological and emotional well-being.

The book has been prompted by the author's personal experiences of and struggles with suffering—especially in relation to relationship breakdowns, mid-life issues, change, meaning, and identity— and his attempts to understand and deal with those issues. It is informed by his own academic knowledge, studies, and readings in psychology, counselling, social sciences, and cultural studies; his professional work, teaching, and training in the fields of counselling and addictions, health, and social care; his personal readings on Buddhism and other religions; and his personal experience, insights, knowledge, reflections, and thoughts on life.

The book is for anyone interested in understanding the human condition, human nature, experience, and behaviour, as well as psychological and emotional suffering, including those who may be seeking self-help in relation to these. Readers may be lay people, students, or researchers in related fields of study (e.g. psychology, social psychology, social sciences, philosophy, cultural studies, anthropology, theology, the arts); social and mental health care practitioners, including counsellors, psychotherapists, psychologists, psychiatrists, social workers; educationists, policy makers, and politicians.

INTRODUCTION

And all our yesterdays have lighted fools
The way to dusty death. Out, out, brief candle,
Life's but a walking shadow, a poor player
That struts and frets his hour upon the stage,
And then is heard no more. It is a tale
Told by an idiot, full of sound and fury
Signifying nothing.

William Shakespeare, *Macbeth* (1606)

We are all busy leading our lives by going to work, paying bills, shopping, maintaining relationships and households, raising families, socialising, spending time on hobbies, holidaying, and relaxing through being entertained by TV, books, cinema, music, sport, etc. But whilst we are busy living, do we ever stop and ask ourselves: *What am I? Why am I doing what I am doing? Why am I thinking what I'm thinking? Why am I feeling what I'm feeling? Why do I suffer? What is the meaning and purpose of life?*

Unless you are a philosopher, psychologist, social scientist, or spiritual guide, more often than not, these questions may arise during personal, familial, and social crises, such as life-threatening illness, bereavement, divorce, relationship breakdown, bankruptcy, redundancy, homelessness, retirement, natural disasters, war, etc. These are times when we suffer and struggle to try to understand and make sense of life and life's events that seem to be unfair and conspire against our happiness and well-being; when we try to cope with existential, psychological and emotional distress and anxiety; or when we may become depressed or develop other mental health problems.

Increasingly, in the postmodern world, the mere experience and feelings of loneliness, isolation, and alienation can cause suffering and can prompt these questions in the individual about the human condition and human nature. During such times of personal crises and in seeking answers to these existential questions, we may seek help from friends, family, GPs, psychologists, psychiatrists, counsellors, religious advisers, or self-help books. But despite, and because of, these varied (and often conflicting) sources of help and the answers they provide, ultimately, we alone must choose which of these rings true, works, and makes sense.

Through the ages man has become more conscious, reflexive, and linguistic. Society has become more complex with the rise of the individual and all the choices open to him or her. This makes the question *Who am I?* increasingly important.

I have a name, gender, ethnicity, class, age, body, family, friends, job, interests, and hobbies. I have a culture and a religion. I have a personality consisting of likes, dislikes, and fears. I have beliefs, values, attitudes, and morals; and I behave and act in the world (mostly!) in accordance with these. I have a history and memories. I have feelings, wishes, urges, drives, and motivations. I am also a citizen, a parent, an employee, a householder, a spouse, etc.

But do these psychosocial parameters reveal, define, constitute, and reflect a cohesive, essential inner me—a real me? Or are they merely constructions grounded in and produced by social, cultural, political, scientific language, discursive practices, and ideology? All of these give me, and society, an illusion of my being an individual—perhaps a handy form of labelling? Constructions give a sense of meaning to my life and a personal and social identity. But at the same time, they give society a means of socio-political-cultural control and exploitation. For example, in a capitalist society, individuals may be seen to be constructed, identified, and treated as consumers with their attendant human values seen as commodities.

Why is it that we as humans suffer psychologically and emotionally? Is this a given or an essential part of the human condition? On what basis do we suffer—what are the mechanisms?

How much is our suffering related to biological, genetic, or evolutionary factors? How much to psychological factors like our thinking, emotions, and behaviour? And how much to the social, cultural, and discursive contexts we live in, or to our spiritual selves?

Do we have to suffer? Quite obviously, we know that most humans do suffer. However, the degree or extent of suffering and its impacts may vary from individual to individual. Suffering may involve feelings, thoughts, memories, images, behaviours, and brain chemistry. It may be natural and the body's way of telling us what's happened. Suffering may help us change and learn from the experience. But if it goes on for too long, then it may become a more serious and chronic problem for us.

Emotional and psychological suffering often relates to attachment and loss. We may lose someone close through bereavement, relationship breakdown, or divorce. We may lose our job, material possessions, or our wealth. Losses can include our health, youth, looks, or sexuality. We may even lose ourselves and our direction or meaning in life.

The effects of suffering can be seen in preverbal babies and in our animal counterparts when a mate, sibling, or parent of a member of the group dies or leaves. Certain behaviours may be observed in the abandoned member like pining, not eating, not communicating with others, or retracing/re-enacting behaviours. Natural (and biological) though these behavioural effects may be: to what degree, in humans, might the personal, social, linguistic, or discursive worlds cause or exacerbate the effects of suffering and hinder the processes of natural or spiritual healing?

In dealing with our suffering, the way we see and what we believe about the human condition, human nature, and the person, may shape how we see and what we believe about ourselves, others, social situations, and events. This in turn, may affect how we respond, feel, behave, and act in the world. Why is it that some people may deal with and get over negative life events or situations better than others? Some individuals may develop a range of psychological conditions such as depression, anxiety, stress, or, more seriously, psychiatric or pathological conditions, including neuroses, psychoses, personality disorders, obsessions, or compulsions. Could it be that, apart from genetic, organic, or pathological underlying factors or determinants, the conception or model (whether tacit or explicit) of the human condition held by the latter group of people, underlies and perpetuates their condition and their suffering? And, could it be the former's model mitigates the effects of negative life events, thereby reducing those individuals' level of suffering? Is our psychological well-being and our level of suffering dependent on the model we live by i.e. how we construe the human condition, human nature, and the person?

Individuals may (consciously, unconsciously, or tacitly) themselves adopt different models of the human condition for their everyday living and being. Because of this, it is of interest to be aware of the range of models adopted and used by mental health professionals for working with clients/patients and the range of models expounded by sociologists, social psychologists, philosophers, cultural studies researchers, and society at large (including religion). There exists major philosophical disagreements between approaches in these disciplines over what the human condition is; how to understand and explain it; and, therefore, how to treat, or remedy, emotional and psychological suffering.

Further, current-day postmodernist/post-structuralist theories question whether there is a stable core to human nature, identity, the self, and the individual, instead positing that we are only subjects of, and constituted in, language and discursive practices. Such subjects are produced by social and cultural institutions, practices, and ideology. Human nature is not nature at all but merely a sociopolitical and sociocultural construction; as is the notion of the self, the individual, or the person.

In support of its critique of essentialist/individual-based approaches to human nature and psychology, the anti-essentialist, postmodernist approach argues that the former has operated on a number of false dualisms or dichotomies. This limits our understanding and perpetuates a number of socially, historically, and culturally constructed illusions about the human condition (i.e. its individual and essential nature). These false dualisms include the separating of, or distinguishing between: (i) the individual and society; (ii) the mind (mental functions) and body (including emotions); (iii) the subject (the person) and the (empirical/material) object; (iv) representation (ideas) and (empirical/material) reality; and (v) agency (individual action) and structure (the environment).

Postmodernism further argues that truth, knowledge, and meaning are situated and are never absolute, fixed, or ending. Therefore, this negates the application of the empirical sciences (including psychology)—and hence the essentialist approach—to the study of human nature.

Philosophically, we can say that the two approaches differ in their conception of reality. Firstly, there is ontology (what exists/is reality) and, secondly, epistemology (how we gain knowledge of what exists/ is reality). Essentialist models (i.e. idealism, and phenomenology), stemming from Plato, posit that reality is located in the conscious mind of the individual (only), in ideas and phenomena and, therefore, give rise to a humanist approach, where the individual is all important, has agency, a core, exists, possesses self and identity, and exerts control over his or her self and their world. Whereas, postmodern/anti-essentialist approaches posit reality is located in language, culture, and the social world, thereby negating the existence/conception of the (essential) individual. For essentialist approaches, therefore, suffering would be located within the person and their individual psychology and for anti-essentialist approaches, located within social, linguistic, cultural, and discursive constructs, narratives, and practices that produce the subject and the possible range of subject positions or discourses available to them.

Further, empirical/scientific approaches (i.e. empiricism and materialism) stemming from Aristotle, posit that reality is located in the empirical/objective world, which is separate to, and of more import than, the subjective world of the individual, the mind, ideas, and phenomena. Therefore, suffering, from this perspective, is to be located in the physiology, biology, and brain chemistry of the individual, vis-à-vis the medical model rather than their subjective world, or in the scientifically observable psychological and behavioural processes of the individual.

Realist approaches (i.e. realism) posit that reality is situated in real-world objects (i.e. social structures, objects, and relations), which have real consequences for people. It is these that underlie and impact on any examination of the human condition. To remedy an individual's suffering requires changing not their mind or brain, but objects, structures, and relations in their external, social world.

Finally, psychodynamic approaches assert that reality and personality are located in the individual and social psyche (i.e. the psychic/unconscious internal world of objects and object relations). The external world is constructed, processed, represented, and emotionally related to, internally and dynamically through various unconscious processes, including projection (the throwing out of bad feelings or parts), introjection (the taking in of good feelings or parts), splitting, phantasies and defences.

Psychic reality and personality is shaped both by early, preverbal development (mother-child relations) and primitive instincts/drives, as well as social morality and norms. A psychologically healthy individual is one who has learned to balance the needs and reality of the external world with the needs of his own internal world and ego (i.e. the depressive position); whereas, an inability to achieve this balance may lead to the paranoid-schizoid position and disorders like the narcissistic personality. Suffering, from this perspective, stems from the individual's unconscious processes or patterns of relating to the world and their ability to psychically and dynamically balance their instincts, drives and the ego's needs with reality and the needs and expectations of society and others (the superego). The psychodynamic approach assumes that the psyche, its processes, structure, and personality are produced in infancy when the helpless, preverbal baby is totally dependent on the mother for meeting its physical and emotional needs, which then carries forth into adulthood. Therefore, an individual adult's experience of suffering reflects and mirrors the suffering they experienced as a baby in relation to their mother and the world around them.

Increasingly, western psychology is looking toward and incorporating eastern philosophical and spiritual approaches to understanding the human condition, the mind, and suffering. Zen Buddhism proposes that the notion of self is an illusion and that our attachment to it underpins all suffering. Most of our everyday thoughts, actions, feelings, emotions, and desires pertain to protecting or satisfying the illusory self and ego. These Buddhist truths may be uncovered through the practices of mindfulness and meditation. Once a person realises, understands, and works with these truths, their suffering may end. First, we need to understand that there is no self, why and from where our painful thoughts and feelings originate, and that they do not define us, and nor are they real. Only then we may become less fearful of them. We can also help to dissipate them and become less overtaken by them. Therefore, we become less anxious, stressed, or depressed. As Brian Thorne (2009) highlights, quoting Ken Wilber (1985):

> I have a body, but I am not a body. I have desires, but I am not my desires. I have emotions, but I am not my emotions. I have thoughts, but I am not my thoughts. I am what remains, a pure centre of awareness, an unmoved witness of all these thoughts, emotions, feelings, and desires. Wilber defines the essence of the human person as spiritual, as transcendent, this self that goes beyond you—the you that is you, but not you.

Thorne (Ibid.) goes on to suggest:

> Humankind cannot ultimately be defined in biological, psychological, or cognitive terms. We are more than that and the mysterious 'moreness' is what makes us human.

Buddhism's view that the self, thoughts, feelings, ego, and the world are illusory is underpinned by its view of reality (Dalai Lama 2011, 90-102, 127-128).

It believes that all phenomena which manifest themselves to our senses and perception, are interconnected/inter-dependent, and therefore, have no identity, autonomous solidity, or ultimate reality and are impermanent:

Buddhist analysis of reality concurs with the conclusions of quantum physics, according to which particles of matter are real while still being devoid of ultimate solidity. Similarly, in Buddhism, the phenomena that exist in interdependence are empty of intrinsic, autonomous existence. (Ibid. 93)

In relation to scientific causality or cause and effect:

Nothing can occur without causes or conditions. A dynamic flux of changing appearances occurs, responding to causes and effects. But that does not mean that we should think there is an original, unchanging, permanent cause, like an organising principle. In a world that is constantly changing, mutations are due to qualities that are inherent in phenomena. (Ibid. 93)

The Dalai Lama gives an analysis of how phenomena may appear real, unchanging, and permanent, but in fact are not (due to moment-to-moment, instant-to-instant change/instability):

Let us take the example of a mountain. Formed thousands of years ago, it represents a continuity in the world of phenomena. Although we can note a relative stability in its appearance on a course level, we must still acknowledge that each of its particles, on a very subtle level, is changing from one instant to the next. Change, on the infinitesimal level, is accompanied in our mind by an appearance of continuity. Yet the continuity thus perceived, is illusory; for nothing remains the same, and no two consecutive instants are alike.

After the example of the mountain, let's take that of the flower. The flower that is blooming today was first a seed, then a bud. These changes of state illustrate the subtle impermanence of every instant, which is the true nature of the flower: it is doomed to rapid destruction. Whether it is a question of a mountain or a flower, we must get used to understanding that the instant a phenomena appears, it carries within it the cause of its own end. (Ibid. 90)

The very existence of the entity known as a flower is questioned by the Dalai Lama. He asserts that it is:

only a collection of characteristics—form, colour, and smell—but no flower exists independent of its appearances. Perceived phenomena exist only from the standpoint of their designation, that is, the names and concepts we attach to them. (Ibid. 91)

As well as the example of a flower, the Dalai Lama also calls into question the reality of the phenomena of time: the truth that the past has no reality because it has no substance and has already occurred. The future has no reality or substance as it does not yet exist. It simply corresponds to subjective projections and anticipations. Only the present is the truth that we experience in the here and now, but it is an elusive reality that does not last long.

We find ourselves in a paradoxical situation in which the present constitutes a border, a limit between a past and a future without any concrete reality. The present is that elusive moment between what no longer exists and what has not yet happened. (Ibid. 91)

In analysing and understanding reality in these ways, the Dalai Lama concludes that we should:

Distinguish two truths: a 'relative truth', which concerns appearance of phenomena, their emergence, their manifestation, and their cessation; and an 'ultimate truth', which recognises the absence of inherent reality in phenomena. (Ibid. 91)

Before we finish this philosophical debate about the nature(s) and conception(s) of what we are, reality, and suffering, certainly for the essentialist approach (as opposed to the post-structuralist/ postmodern), it is important to discuss in a little more detail the mind-body problem, or the problem of mind and brain—the relationship between mind (consciousness) and neurophysiological processes, in particular, brain activity (Gross 1993, 45-48).

It was the seventeenth century French philosopher, Descartes, who originally separated mind and body into this dualism as captured in his famous 'cogito ergo sum' ('I think, therefore I am') formulation. This approach assumes that the mind and body, or brain, are fundamentally and qualitatively different—the brain being reduced to a machine, which is being driven by the non-physical/non-material mind (or soul), the essence of man. If this is assumed to be true, then how are we to understand the relationship between the mind and body (or brain)?

The two major solutions to this problem, as outlined by Gross (Ibid.)—from the dualism perspective—are firstly, that the mind (i.e. the mental—let's call it 'M') and the body/brain (i.e. the physical—let's say 'P') are causally related. This can be in either (i) both directions (vis-à-vis interactionism) e.g. mind over matter and psychosomatic problems (M→P); or mind altering hallucinogenic drugs and brain damage/surgery affecting intelligence/personality (P→M); or, (ii) in one direction only, from P to M (vis-à-vis epiphenomenalism). Albeit, that mental processes here are regarded as only non-causal by-products of physical processes. But as Gross points out, how can something physical and spatial (i.e. brain/body) influence something that is non-physical and non-spatial (i.e. mind), and vice versa? Where does the interaction occur?

A second solution for dualism is that the mind and body are correlated, but causally independent (vis-à-vis psychophysical parallelism). In this solution, mental and physical events occur simultaneously like two synchronised clocks, but do not causally influence each other. 'There is a one-to-one correspondence between how a stimulus is perceived and how it is represented in the brain, a correspondence called by Gestalt psychologists, "isomorphism"'(Ibid.). But the problem here is that there are no simple correlations to be found! For example, 'depression could be associated with a variety of physical states and, conversely, the same physical state could be associated with a number of psychological states' (Ibid.).

An alternative solution to dualism and its mind-body problem is 'monism' (Ibid.), where either (i) physical events are reducible to mental ones (vis-à-vis idealism and phenomenology, as discussed earlier), i.e. reality is represented as ideas and experience only in our heads; or, (ii) mental events are reducible to physical ones (vis-à-vis materialism, also as discussed earlier) i.e. reality is located only in physical phenomena, and therefore, all mental/psychical states including consciousness are located organically, in the brain, or are processes of the brain itself (vis-à-vis identity theory).

So, what can we learn about what we are and why we suffer from these scientific approaches to mind and body/brain? Clearly, there is both a physical and mental component to the human condition and suffering. Our consciousness and experience, our behaviours, and our realities are produced by and contingent upon, both brain (physical) and psychological (mental) processes. However, which component (mind or body) causes, or precedes/determines which, and is, therefore, of greater significance, is still contested. Our suffering may be located in both our brain/body as well as our conscious, experiencing mind. Therefore, to reduce suffering may require both physical and psychological interventions (i.e. on both the brain and the body as well as the mind, respectively). Traditionally, medical interventions (i.e. drugs) may be used to change brain states; whereas talking therapies (e.g. counselling and psychotherapy), may be used to change the mind. Alternative therapies such as yoga, meditation, relaxation, reflexology, massage, and acupuncture may be used to effect changes in both body and mind.

However, another scientific view, that of behaviourism, which we shall discuss further on, departs radically from the mind/body approach altogether, and argues that the mind is irrelevant (regarding it as a black box); positing that only external, observable (conditioned or learned) behaviour is relevant in understanding human psychology/nature. And as we have seen above, spiritual approaches may yet again identify other, metaphysical or transpersonal factors, over and above the mind/body approach.

And so, what exactly am I, and why do I suffer? I will first look at my physical origins; secondly, my innate, biological, psychological, and evolutionary origins and properties; thirdly, my spiritual dimension; fourthly, my sociocultural, linguistic and discursive self; fifthly, myself, as located within the real world.

THE PHYSICAL WORLD

Cosmic Man

For me, it is far better to grasp the Universe as it really is than to persist in delusion, however satisfying and reassuring.

If we long to believe that the stars rise and set for us, that we are the reason there is a Universe, does science do us a disservice in deflating our conceits?

Who are we? We find that we live on an insignificant planet of a humdrum star lost in a galaxy tucked away in some forgotten corner of a universe in which there are far more galaxies than people.

Carl Sagan

Physically, I am matter, stardust. I am made up of chemicals and properties from the beginning of the universe, the Big Bang, which occurred 13.7 billion years ago. Therefore, I am quite a ripe old age! I am a speck, or a mere point, moving within, and governed by, a space-time dimension. However, as yet, particle physics is still working on why mass, weight, or physical form—my body and everything else in the universe—exists; because at the sub-atomic level, using the standard model theory, particles have no mass! Just like at the time of the Big Bang.

Scientists, using the Large Hadron Collider (LHC), think they have found the key particle—the Higgs boson, or the God particle. This may prove that an electromagnetic field, the Higgs Field, exists. The Higgs Field is thought to produce mass in massless particles that travel through it. This will then explain why my physical body and anything with mass in the world exists.

In relation to the universe, I am miniscule in size. The visible universe is estimated to be a sphere with a diameter of ninety-three billion light years. Our star (the sun), is one of thirty to seventy billion trillion stars, organised into more than eighty billion galaxies, of which ours, the Milky Way, is one. These are themselves organised into groups, clusters, and super-clusters, with the Milky Way being one of forty galaxies in our group.

Looking at my physical being, then, as being composed of universal matter and energy originating in the Big Bang; matter and energy which cannot be destroyed (only changed from one form to another): I am, and have always been, even before my birth, and always will be, even after my death, an inextricable part of the physical universe—the cosmos. How then can I be lonely? How can I fear death? Through sharing the same cosmic matter, I am part of every human being and the whole of the natural and physical world. Bearing in mind my infinitesimal size, in relation to the universe, how big are my problems? How big is my suffering and my unhappiness? How big can my ego be and the importance I attach to myself? Birth, death, ego, and suffering may be seen to be man-made. Earthly concepts and properties based on the material and cultural world, which, whilst giving meaning to our human condition, at the same time imprison and limit us.

Evolutionary Man: The Human Animal

Most of what we strive for in our modern life uses the apparatus of goal seeking that was originally set up to seek goals in the state of nature.

Richard Dawkins (1995)

We are survival machines—robot vehicles—blindly programmed to preserve the selfish molecules known as genes.

Richard Dawkins (1976)

Humans and other animals, reason, decide, and behave by virtue of computational devices embodied in neural tissue. Therefore, a complete causal explanation of any behaviour—rational or otherwise—necessarily invokes theories about the architecture of these computational devices. The rationality of a behaviour is irrelevant to its cause or explanation.

Leda Cosmides (1994)

Form follows function. The properties of an evolved mechanism reflect the structure of the task it evolved to solve.

Leda Cosmides (Ibid.)

As a biological organism, I evolved from early cell life, called the amoeba; through to primitive man, Homo habilis, two million years ago. Then I evolved into Homo erectus, 1.8 million years ago; and into Homo sapiens, two hundred and fifty thousand years ago.

My primitive forebears were born with a range of pre-existing, preverbal, innate capacities and attributes designed for survival, such as fleeing, fighting, foraging, hunting, and reproducing. This also included emotions, instincts, drives, motivation, intention, perception, problem solving, intelligence, language acquisition, memory, self-awareness (or reflexivity), and consciousness. These innate capacities manifested themselves and culminated in the invention of tools, which further developed these capacities.

My earliest forebears lived in groups as hunter-gatherers or nomads; and so, early social and cultural life was established. As a human, with reproductive organs, I am able to procreate and hence, pass on my genes to future generations. In this way, I am replenishing and perpetuating the human species.

My forebears believed that natural phenomena, such as day and night, rainfall, fire, the sun and moon, planting and crop growth, were magical and mystical, or produced by a higher or a more powerful force. These forces included God(s), spirits, etc. Science—as developed over the centuries and superseding religion—has provided me with rational explanations for most natural phenomena, and increased my knowledge and understanding, and my use of these, to master myself and my environment. However, early myths and beliefs still remain in my unconscious or psyche. Societal evidence for this can be seen in our continuing beliefs in religion, miracles, fate, paganism, magic, the occult, astrology, tarot cards, the supernatural, witch doctors, shamanism, complementary medicines and therapies, spiritual healing—the list goes on!

Carl Jung (1996), the Swiss psychiatrist, posited that the sum of human experience—in the form of archetypes (akin to Plato's philosophy of ideas), and dating back as far as prehistory, is stored in our memory and in the collective unconscious, which is innate, heritable and evolutionary. Archetypes (e.g. the father, hero, wise old man, knight, princess, dragon, witch, and stranger) are all found in literature. This literature including folklore, fables, and fairy tales, still persists, and permeates the modern social and cultural psyche. For example, in our political and religious leaders we may unconsciously regard and accept them as the father or the king archetypes; as wise, all-powerful, all-knowing, caring, protecting, rewarding, punishing, or in control. As for the foreigner in our country, we may unconsciously regard him as the stranger, the outsider, and as a threat or danger to our community, country, kingdom, or tribe of which someone may be wary. In western romantic love we still may unconsciously believe that we need to be looking for a beautiful princess or handsome prince to be our perfect partner with whom we will forever be in love and live together happily ever after in our castle.

Jung also posited, in his theory on anima and animus, that within our unconscious minds we hold a perfect representation of the qualities of feminine or masculine, depending on our opposite gender, based on our mothers, fathers, brothers, sisters, etc. Therefore, in finding and marrying a woman, I may actually be marrying my anima—my idealised, unconscious, representation or composite of the feminine, based on my mother and sister—and not the actual woman! And in the same way, a woman may marry her animus. Is it small wonder then that many relationships fail or break down, with unrealistic hopes dashed, and unrealistic expectations and needs unmet? Each partner, unconsciously, may be looking for things that are not in each other, but in their own unconscious minds! Is it any wonder that we feel let down by our leaders—politicians, teachers, managers, etc.—when our needs and expectations, based on our unconscious archetypes, are not met or realised?

I have a neurological and neurochemical substrate controlling my central nervous system (i.e. essentially my brain and spine). A range of neurotransmitters (chemical messengers, transmitting impulses across neurons via synapses in my brain) and hormones, which are linked to changes in my environment, body, and neural patterns in my brain, cause me to experience emotions and feelings, which motivate me to behave in certain ways. They register pleasure and reward in my brain. This may relate to things like sexual intercourse, eating, physical exercise, social interaction and risk taking.

For example, serotonin makes me feel good; dopamine makes me feel pleasure, well-being and euphoria; anandamide gives me the feeling of bliss; endorphins, released at times of physical injury, act as natural painkillers; GABA reduces excessive brain activity and reduces anxiety; and oxytocin is linked to human and sexual relationships, mating and maternal behaviours including social recognition, bonding and trust. Adrenalin (epinephrine) and noradrenalin (norepinephrine) are energising and rapidly prepare my body for action when danger threatens or in emergency situations (i.e. a fight or flight mode, or short-term stress reactions). They boost the supply of oxygen and glucose to my brain and muscles, while suppressing non-emergency bodily processes (like digestion), and they increase heart rate and dilate my pupils for acute vision.

Am I essentially a primitive man, a sophisticated animal? All my behaviours, brain chemistry and psychology are primarily linked to survival and in perpetuating my genes. Also included would be fighting over or finding food and shelter, finding (and fighting for) a mate, procreating, and raising offspring. Perhaps striving, or fighting, to become the alpha male, leader, or someone with ultimate power and authority over others. At a social level, banding together and identifying with chosen groups to ensure our mutual survival, such as my relatives, friends, community, football team, country, or religion. As well as support them, I may fight, or go to war, and kill for them, too. We have only to look at the scramble for resources at the sales during recession, at the fuel pumps, in the stock market, and in the job centre; the practice of Machiavellian work practices, nepotism, racism, bullying, and helicopter parenting.

Are my emotions and feelings—and, therefore, my motivation and behaviour—merely driven and determined by changing, neural patterns and chemicals in my brain? Chemicals that tell me when I am happy, when I'm sad, when I'm in love, when I'm frightened, when and who I want to mate or have sexual intercourse with, when I am angry and frustrated, and when I should become aggressive or violent?

Is suffering to do with which chemicals I have or do not have, or the levels of these in my brain? When I hunt for love, find it, and live with it, I may become ecstatically happy; but when I lose it, I may become desperately sad or depressed, unmotivated and despondent—withdrawing—as does a heroin addict, from the related feel-good drugs in my brain.

From this perspective, then, a range of everyday behaviours can be explained in terms of wanting to increase, boost, or stimulate feel-good chemicals in our brains, such as falling in love, shopping, eating, drinking coffee, having sex, drinking alcohol, taking drugs, gambling, listening to music, watching films, exercising, driving fast cars, thrill seeking, and risk taking. When done to excess, some of us may become dependent on, or addicted to, these activities resulting in our developing a problem.

Is the extent of my suffering and unhappiness linked to my meeting and acting in accordance with my biological needs and drives? Thereby, ensuring my brain chemistry is balanced and optimised? Should I laugh more, find love, engage in sexual activity, seek thrills, exercise more, give more vent to my anger and emotions? Psychiatry's and/or medicine's approach to treating unhappiness, or depression and anxiety, has been to administer drugs that will alter brain chemistry and activity (e.g. slow it down or speed it up) because it sees emotional and psychological states as linked to these. Alternative non-medical approaches to addressing brain chemistry may lie in, for example, exercising, reflexology and Tai Chi. As well, other approaches could involve therapies such as laughter, drama, art, aromatherapy, massage, meditation, and talking therapies (e.g. counselling and psychotherapy), all of which are designed to vent or discharge emotion or re-structure our thinking and behavioural patterns.

Suffering, essentially, involves my conscious mind, my emotions, and feelings. But where do emotions and feelings actually come from? What are they?

> He jests at scars that never felt a wound.
> **William Shakespeare,** *Romeo and Juliet* (1595)

Antonio Damasio (1999), the eminent neuroscientist, theorises on the evolutionary nature of emotions and consciousness. Emotions, he asserts, are 'cognitive representations of body states,' (vis-à-vis the Somatic Marker Mechanism, or SMM) or 'nerve activation patterns' that correspond to the state of the internal world, which act as inputs to the brain (specifically, working memory), and from which our behaviour can be modified accordingly. For example, an attacker or predatory animal coming toward us would register in our body and working memory/brain as the emotion of fear, and we may, therefore, flee or stand and fight. Therefore, emotions are essential for the human organism to recognise and register external input and situations in order to act. Damasio differentiates between emotions and feelings. Whereas emotions, which are designed for survival, are naturally occurring biological body states operating outside of consciousness, feelings are our conscious (and sociolinguistic) interpretation of emotions. Feelings alert us to our underlying emotions. So, using the example of the base emotion of fear, we may have feelings of being frightened, consternation, surprise, bewilderment, and confusion, etc.

Bruce Charlton (2000) suggests that emotions, the SMM, and language are linked to social intelligence and human consciousness; which evolved in early man, primarily, for dealing competitively with other humans in social situations, or through social tasks (i.e. one person being able to guess at what another is thinking in relation to their own thinking) in the face of differential chances of reproductive success. The myriad other functions and uses of consciousness and language following on from their most primitive origins, are regarded as epiphenomena, or, accidental by-products not related to the evolutionary necessity for these capacities. What Charlton is alluding to is that the many social uses we put our social intelligence and human consciousness to in the modern and postmodern world are not natural, but man made, and therefore, not used for that which they were originally designed. In terms of suffering, then, is our preoccupation with ourselves as individuals. Are feelings such as introspection, worrying, obsessional thinking, anxiety, stress, depression, and suffering man made? Are they a sociolinguistic-cultural construction? Perhaps they are a form of narcissism?

The growth in psychology, psychotherapy, counselling, and humanism along with other movements relating to personal development or growth and self-actualisation, bears witness to this. The arts, including music, literature, and poetry often relate to the artist's introspection of personal feelings, emotions, suffering, and angst. The media, too, creates or constructs personas or personalities, which perpetuates further, our obsession with examining and commenting on the individual. The world of advertising and consumerism constructs us as types or categories of individuals, with certain needs, wants, and desires in order to sell to us. Through ideology, political parties construct and see us as certain types of people with certain values, beliefs, morals, and natures.

From the perspective of evolutionary biology and neuroscience, then, the nature of my suffering may possibly be understood in the following terms.

An external event occurs such as my partner leaves me, my spouse dies, I am physically assaulted or wounded, a threat to my life is made, I lose my job, I am diagnosed with a life-threatening illness, or I become bankrupt. The organism responds in a natural, biological, or evolutionary way through the SMM. Then, an appropriate unconscious bodily emotional response occurs, nerve activation patterns relay this to my brain into my working memory, a cognitive representation is made of my bodily emotional state, and an appropriate behavioural response is made. The way my conscious mind is made aware of what is going on in my body and brain is through the feelings relayed to/felt by me. At this stage, I might prolong my suffering and turn it into a chronic condition since my conscious mind is a sociocultural entity/process. It is here where I am socially and culturally aware of myself; where I hold my values, beliefs, and attitudes; and where I learn a range of socially accepted and constructed responses consisting behaviours and actions. It is here where my ego lies, my self-interest/self-obsession; engagement with, and attachment to, the material world. I may choose to become depressed. As a depressed person, I may wallow in self-pity, cry a lot, isolate myself, stay indoors, not see friends or go to work, etc. I may become an anxious person and exhibit worry or fear, or exaggerate or magnify things. I may become a stressed person exhibiting the inability to cope, with signs of confusion, shortness in temper, etc. I may designate myself as the victim and exhibit the range of behaviours that befit this construct. These socially constructed personhoods or positions may be social markers letting people know of my particular emotional state, or giving me some kind of social advantage by garnering sympathy, extra resources, support, or comfort. This could act as a way out of facing the world or reality, such as not having to go to work, look after myself, meet people, or make difficult decisions or choices.

Whereas, emotions are appropriate, naturally occurring, evolutionary-based responses to immediate external situations, our suffering may be a chronic and dysfunctional social response to these emotions via internally or self-induced dysfunctional feelings and thinking. These dysfunctional feelings may involve negative, irrational, or obsessional thoughts, which keep the emotions (i.e. the SMM) alive, even in the absence of the immediate threat that triggered the initial emotion(s). In other words, we may continuously re-live the event in our minds and, therefore, maintain the initial SMM.

Dan Millman's character, a Zen master called Socrates (*Way of the Peaceful Warrior*, 2000, 52-53), makes a useful distinction in understanding the difference between the naturally appropriate and responding evolutionary brain and the epiphenomenaeic, phantom-like, mind (where our socially constructed feelings may possibly originate):

> You have a brain that directs the body, stores information, and plays with that information. We refer to the brain's abstract processes as the 'intellect'. The brain and the mind are not the same. The brain is real; the mind isn't. Mind is an illusory reflection of cerebral fidgeting. It comprises all the random, uncontrolled thoughts that bubble into awareness from the

subconscious. Mind is an obstruction, an aggravation. It is a kind of evolutionary mistake in the human being, a primal weakness in the human experiment. I have no use for the mind.

The brain can be a tool. It can recall phone numbers, solve math puzzles, or create poetry. In this way, it works for the rest of the body, like a tractor. But when you can't stop thinking of that math problem, or phone number, or when troubling thoughts and memories arise without your intent, it's not your brain working, but your mind wandering. Then the mind controls you; then the tractor has run wild . . . Your thoughts are like wild monkeys stung by a scorpion.

In terms of a remedy for the process of suffering outlined here using the SMM model, it would appear that I would need to ensure that I expose myself to positive external events and stimuli, thus creating appropriately positive emotional states (through the SMM), resulting in appropriately positive feelings; and, therefore, appropriately positive thinking/thoughts, which lead to appropriately positive behaviours and actions.

Although I have argued here for a socially constructed, self-imposing, determining, and self-interested dimension to dealing with feelings and the suffering this may lead to, there are other mediating factors, based on individual psychology, which psychiatry and psychology may consider as disorders linked to thinking, feelings, emotions, personality, and moods. Some people may be cognitively predisposed to thinking negatively about themselves or events in the world. Some may be neurotic and prone to experiencing negative affect, emotions, or feelings. Additionally, there clearly may be organic, or pathological, conditions underlying a person's suffering, such as a range of psychoses (like schizophrenia), neuroses and personality disorders, and neurological conditions and those relating to brain damage.

It is to the psychological model of human nature that we will turn to now.

Psychological Man

How now, my lord, why do you keep alone,
Of sorriest fancies your companions making,
Using those thoughts which should indeed have died
With them they think on? Things without all remedy
Should be without regard—what's done, is done.

William Shakespeare, *Macbeth* (1606)

Present fears
Are less than horrible imaginings.

(Ibid.)

There is nothing either good or bad, but thinking makes
it so.

William Shakespeare, *Hamlet* (1601)

Psychology asserts that my mind and the mental or cognitive processes of my brain are the substratum of all my personal and social behaviours, feelings, and emotions, language acquisition, memory, learning, problem solving, and intelligence (IQ).

Through a combination of biology and experiencing the world (via my senses), my early life experiences, relationships and socialisation, I acquire a personal, individual, and social psychology, such as my thoughts, attitudes, beliefs, and feelings about myself and the world. These underpin and explain my personal and social behaviour. They are measurable and testable properties and processes, which can also predict my behaviour in given situations. From this perspective, then, my suffering (negative, distressing feelings, thoughts, emotions, and behaviour) stems from the fixed beliefs and attitudes I hold of myself and the world—the way I think.

Psychology also asserts that I have a personality, which includes enduring and fixed traits, dispositions, and propensities, predisposing and compelling me to think, feel, and behave in certain predictable, pre-determined ways and define me as a specific personality type.

The Myers-Briggs Type Indicator—MBTI (1962)—based on Carl Jung's Psychological Types (Jung 1921), makes the assumption that people are born with, or develop preferred ways of thinking and acting and posits that personality types are based on four dichotomous dimensions: extraversion-introversion (EI), sensing-intuition (SN), thinking-feeling (TF), judging-perceiving (JP). Combinations of these preferences (e.g. ENTJ or INTJ) go on to yield sixteen possible personality types.

Extraversion signifies a focus on, or preference for, the external world of action, behaviour, objects and people, all of which energise the extrovert. Introversion focuses on the internal world of reflection and ideas. The external world drains the introvert of energy.

In these terms, it may be seen that the introvert may suffer due to their propensity for mulling over or obsessing about things, whereas, the extravert moves on and interacts with the external world. However, conversely, it may be that due to the need to be engaged more widely with the social world (i.e. people and things) and take more risks, the extravert may be prone to more emotional ups and downs, with less time to reflect, think, and learn before acting the next time. The introvert, less frequently, lays themselves open to emotionally risky situations (e.g. relationships, social interactions, experiences), but then, they may also be less likely to experience positive social interactions.

When relating to the external world, some people/personality types may prefer to perceive it (preferring to use either their senses or intuition), and some may prefer to judge it (preferring to use either their thinking or their feelings). Could it be the case that the latter may be more prone to suffering, since they would spend more time judging or deciding, thinking, and feeling about events, rather than just perceiving them?

Zen Buddhism stresses how the discriminating mind can lead to suffering; whereas, the mind that just perceives and then lets go of thoughts and feelings may experience less suffering.

The British psychologist, Hans Eysenck (1947) put forward a theory of personality that was considered more robust and scientific than the MBTI. It was based on physiology, biology, and genetics, and suggested that we are born with certain temperaments. He divided these temperaments into two categories: extraversion/introversion, and neuroticism/stability.

In general, neuroticism refers to a tendency to experience negative emotions, and extraversion, a tendency to enjoy positive events, especially social. The two categories yield four personality types: (i) stable extraverts (possessing sanguine qualities such as outgoing, talkative, responsive, easygoing, lively, carefree, leadership); (ii) unstable extraverts (possessing choleric qualities such as touchy, restless, excitable, changeable, impulsive, irresponsible); (iii) stable introverts (possessing phlegmatic qualities such as calmness, even temper, reliable, controlled, peaceful, thoughtful, careful, passive); and (iv) unstable introverts (possessing melancholic qualities such as quiet, reserved, pessimistic, sober, rigid, anxious, moody).

Eysenck later added a further category of psychoticism/socialisation, associated with a person's vulnerability to psychotic episodes (breaks with reality), characterised by aggression, tough-mindedness, nonconformity, inconsideration, recklessness, hostility, anger, and impulsiveness.

Eysenck went on to elicit personality traits associated with each temperament category. For psychoticism, these are: aggressive, assertive, egocentric, unsympathetic, manipulative, achievement-oriented, dogmatic, masculine, and tough-minded. For extraversion, these are: sociable, irresponsible, dominant, lacking reflection, sensation seeking, impulsive, risk taking, expressive, and active. For neuroticism, these are: anxious, depressed, feelings of guilt, low self-esteem, tense, moody, hypochondriac, lack of autonomy, and obsessive.

Eysenck links personality types to physiology, biology and genetics. For example, the brain's cortical arousal level in extraverts is chronically lower than the optimal level (for maximum performance) and, therefore, they need to increase this through external stimulation. For introverts, arousal is chronically high and they, therefore, need to decrease external stimulation to bring it down to the optimal level. Neuroticism—inherited genetically—is based on activation thresholds in the sympathetic nervous system or visceral brain—the part of the brain that is responsible for the fight-or-flight response in the face of danger. People with low activation thresholds may be unable to inhibit or control their emotional reactions to even minor stressors and, therefore, experience negative affect (or feelings). Whereas, those with high activation thresholds have good emotional control and only experience negative affect in relation to major stressors.

Psychoticism is linked to levels of dopamine (and other chemicals in the brain) as well as high levels of testosterone.

Could it, therefore, be that people who are neurotic will suffer more, since their brain's activation threshold for danger, and even minor stressors, is low? They perceive more of the world and external events as dangerous, threatening, and stressful. However, this does not eliminate, altogether, suffering in even those who have higher activation thresholds; it just takes a higher, more serious level of danger or stress to cause them to suffer.

Additionally, in terms of the four personality types discussed above, although unstable extraverts may have higher activation thresholds, due to their restlessness, excitability, changeability, impulsivity, irresponsibility, risk taking, sensation seeking, and lack of reflection, they may get into situations in life that may eventually cause them suffering, too, such as gambling, alcohol, drugs, sexual relationships, and crime.

In a similar way, for people whose temperaments and traits align more toward psychoticism (on the psychoticism-socialisation dimension), their aggressiveness, egotism, lack of sympathy, tendency toward manipulation, and possible breaks with reality may also get them into negative or damaging social situations in life, which may lead them to suffer.

In general, unstable introverts and/or neurotic people, are more inclined to be pessimistic, anxious, depressed, obsessive, lacking in self-esteem, and may obviously, therefore, be prone to suffering more frequently.

Although the approach of personality types appears to be deterministic, with no way out for the individual born into their type, cognitive-behavioural therapies (CBT), to which we will now turn, have been relatively successful in their attempt to alter the way people think, behave, and feel.

Man as Information Processor

Doctor: Not so sick, my lord,
As she is troubled with thick-coming fancies
That keep her from her rest.

Macbeth: Cure her of that:
Canst thou not minister to a mind diseased,
Pluck from the memory a rooted sorrow,
Raze out the written troubles of the brain,
And with some sweet oblivious antidote
Cleanse the stuffed bosom of that perilous stuff
Which weighs upon the heart?

William Shakespeare, *Macbeth* (1606)

The mind is a neural computer.

Steven Pinker (1997)

Through being able to simulate and replicate human cognitive processes, using Artificial Intelligence (AI), cognitive psychology/ science concludes and asserts that I am essentially an intelligent, rational, efficient, information processing machine. My brain, like a computer, consisting of a central processing unit, short-term working and long-term (hard drive) memory, stores all logical processes; schema (or algorithms) for recognising external inputs, assimilating/integrating them, whilst growing or elaborating the schema to accommodate new knowledge and learning. All decisions to act are calculated, are based on rationality, and are designed to maximise personal gain, profit, and advantage (in all its manifestations) and minimise personal loss and disadvantage.

But do computers have feelings, emotions and consciousness? Do they suffer? Are we, as humans, rational? What about our irrational behaviour and our unconscious? Is my suffering due to faulty programming or faulty algorithms (software) or hardware (my brain or neural networks)? The character Spock (from *Star Trek*) comes very much to mind when one thinks of humans in this way. And what of the human need, and capacity, for creating meaning via avenues such as love, culture, aesthetics, or personal and social identities? Human endeavours in music, art, poetry, drama, literature, film and pop culture, etc. all bear witness to this and attempt to capture, describe, and reflect the subjective experience of being human. And do computers have a spiritual, metaphysical, and transpersonal dimension? Do they believe in a computer God? Do computers have personal histories, narratives, and identities? Humans appear to need to have these to describe who they are and their life history.

Cognitive science/psychology may help us to understand and explain the automatic mental processing that occurs in our brains— memory, calculations, language, problem solving, perception of objects, representation, etc.—but may be of limited use in understanding the human condition, human experience, meaning, emotions, and feelings as we know them. These may be seen as merely, further cognitive processes; or 'by-products' of cognitive processes i.e. 'epiphenomena'. This concurs with the evolutionary biology perspective of Bruce Charlton, as discussed earlier.

Notwithstanding these limitations, a branch of humanist psychology, counselling, and therapy—which acknowledges the existence of human emotions and feelings and their effects on behaviour—has utilised the cognitive approach in treating people with psychological and emotional problems.

Approaches like Cognitive Behavioural Therapy (CBT), Cognitive Therapy (CT) and Rational Emotive Behaviour Therapy (REBT) assert that the way we think, affects how we feel and consequently, how we behave. Certain patterns of irrational beliefs and assumptions about ourselves, others, situations, and the world, and negative, automatic, thoughts (e.g. awfulising, magnifying, overgeneralising, selective abstraction, dichotomous thinking) cause certain emotional, and therefore, behavioural responses in us. Therapy involves challenging and changing these irrational or dysfunctional thoughts, beliefs, and assumptions into more rational and functional ones, thereby leading to more positive emotions and behaviours.

So using this analysis, I suffer because I have suffering-related thoughts. If I eliminate or change these thoughts, I shall cease, or reduce my suffering. Interestingly, and perhaps surprisingly, this approach has much in common with Zen Buddhism (as discussed earlier); which also aligns suffering and emotions with mind and thinking, and believes by eliminating and/or controlling these elements, you may eliminate and/or control suffering. Additionally, thinking and suffering relate to our attachment to a self-concept and ego and to material objects and possessions in the world. Anything which threatens the existence of these will cause us to suffer emotional and psychological pain. Again, surprisingly, the successful use of drugs in psychiatry for treating thought-related disorders (anxiety, depression, OCD, etc.) indicates the primacy of thinking in relation to suffering.

Further evidence for thinking being related to psychological well-being can be found in the use of the Health Realisation (HR) or Mind, Thought, Consciousness/Innate Health (MTC/IH) model as used within Principal Based Correctional Counselling (PBCC), as applied to the fields of delinquency and youth violence, positive youth development, community empowerment, school violence, and correctional counselling, criminality/offending and probation (Kelly 2011).

This model proposes that a person's individual subjective experience results from interplay between the principles of mind, thought, and consciousness: (i) mind is the formless, universal, intelligent energy that constantly flows through all human beings and powers the human faculties of thought and consciousness to produce each individual's personal reality or unique life experience; (ii) thought is 'the human capacity to use the formless energy of mind to create an infinitely variable personal reality to express unique life, the individual human power, or ability to create one's experienced reality. It describes the mental imaging ability of human beings, the ongoing creation of all experience via mental activity' (Kelly 2011, 141). And (iii) consciousness is 'the energy of mind that transforms thought or mental activity into subjective experience through the five physical senses. Since people use thought to create mental images, these representations appear real to them as they merge with the faculty of consciousness and register as sensory experience. Consciousness allows the recognition of form—form being the expression of thought. Consciousness uses thought to inform the senses, resulting in each individual's ongoing experienced reality. Consciousness also allows people to recognise the fact that they are creating their ongoing personal reality from the inside out through thought and their senses' (Ibid.).

Further, the model proposes that our highest levels (or purest states) of consciousness contain innate health, wisdom, or intelligent, responsive thought processes. Innate health includes 'well-being, self-esteem, humility, compassion, peace of mind, common sense, and deep human feelings, such as gratitude, exhilaration, and compassion. People can only lose touch with this innate healthy functioning by thinking themselves away from it' (Ibid.). This is always available to be drawn out, drawn upon, and re-kindled. So consciousness can experience innate health, as well as pain and misery. Whatever level of consciousness a person experiences at any given moment depends on the quality of their thinking, which consciousness neutrally takes in and enlivens.

In summary, 'consciousness allows people to: (i) experience whatever they are thinking as their personal reality; and (ii) view their psychological functioning from an impersonal or objective stance' (Ibid.).

So how does thinking affect psychological well-being? According to the MTC/IH model, there are two types of thinking:

(i)   Natural Thinking (NT)—an innate, generic, intelligent, automatic thinking we are all born with, which requires no conscious effort and no stress factor. It produces all the positive psychological experiences associated with mental health. 'It is unfailingly responsive to the moment, providing people with sensory data appropriate to their immediate needs and goals. It is the human default system, surfacing automatically when peoples' minds quiet or clear, when they stop trying to think' (Kelly 2011, 142).

(ii) Personal thinking (PT)—a conditioned, deliberate, learned way of thinking, which requires effort and active concentration to hold certain thoughts in place in order to learn and perform skills and solve problems. 'It is totally restricted to memory and always and only useful for applying known variables to known formulae' (Ibid.).

As it requires effort, PT always has a stress factor—even when used appropriately—and can cause fatigue and symptoms of burnout when overused. PT can be abused through overuse or misuse and can result in considerable psychological dysfunction and 'all misuses of PT are learned, varied, and over time become habitual' (Ibid.). The distress caused by misusing PT is related to 'the painful nature of the thoughts or memories that people choose to dwell on or re-think. Common misuses include worrying, thinking ambivalently, perfectionist thinking, thinking judgementally, obsessive thinking, angry thinking, and egoistic thinking, or using personal thought to create the illusion that self-esteem has to be earned'. According to PBCC, 'the overuse and misuse of personal thinking is the source of all human stress and distress' (Ibid.).

Therefore, in being psychologically healthy, PBCC asserts that optimal human thinking consists of a balanced movement (back and forth) between a spontaneous reliance on NT and the implementation of PT when appropriate. 'When people trust NT to guide them, they automatically receive prompts (i.e. responsive thoughts) to move in and out of PT when necessary without getting stuck in the personal mode' (Ibid.).

PBCC proposes that human feelings are a reliable, in-built self-monitoring system, or barometer, which let us know in each moment whether we are using our thinking in our best interest or against ourselves. In the same way that pain alerts us to physical malfunction, painful feelings signal to us some abuse of thought. 'The greater the psychological pain, the further people have moved away from their innate health, wisdom, pure consciousness and optimal thinking' (Ibid.).

PBCC believes that psychological distress and dysfunctionality occur when someone is not aware of (or under-utilises) NT and solely relies on PT; which they view as the prominent, if not exclusive, thought process and which they have learned to habitually abuse. Dysfunctional behaviour, therefore, can be seen as a person's 'way of reacting or attempting to cope with the distorted perceptions and insecure feelings they experience when they: (1) abuse PT and obscure their innate responsive thought process; and (2) don't recognise that the abuse of thought is the source of their unsettling experience' (Ibid.).

Also, PBCC asserts that 'the frequency of dysfunctional behaviour is determined by: (1) how far and how often a person moves away from his/her innate, healthy thought process; and (2) a person's level of understanding how thought works to create his/her experienced reality from inside-out' (Kelly 2011, 143). Therefore, to improve people's psychological functioning, well-being, and behaviour is to 'facilitate a shift in the way they relate to and use their ability to think' and 'to teach them to look before thought content, to the manner in which they create and then experience the products of their thinking, to produce lasting change by teaching them how to better use and relate to their thinking ability' (Ibid.). These realisations are referred to by PBCC, as 'thought recognition' (Ibid.).

Kelly's research (2011) involving PBCC, evidenced predicted improvement in psychological well-being and more functional behaviour in probationers through their increased levels in thought recognition (through being given eight to twenty hours of PBCC counselling).

Pransky (1997) offers three possible explanations for these findings, namely that greater thought recognition may lead to: (1) a heightened sense of control, as people have more control over their thinking than over their external environment; (2) a heightened level of understanding life experiences that previously may have been confusing or frightening; (3) an increased capacity to view things in a balanced fashion, leading to a more philosophical outlook on life (Kelly 2011, 144). Kelly also offers a further possible explanation: that of mindfulness (vis-à-vis enhanced attention or awareness in the present moment). Kelly (2011, 145) cites a range of researches into psychological health and its indicators which offer consensus that:

> More mindful individuals experience their lives in a less judgemental and defensive manner, typically allowing their

thoughts (positive and negative) to flow through their mind without taking personally or attaching them to the self.

(Heppner et al. 2008)

Thoughts of rejection, insult, loss, and trauma appear to pass through the minds of such individuals without initiating symptoms of acute stress, threats to self-esteem, or triggering defensive outbursts.

(Hodgins & Knee 2002)

More mindful individuals seem to view their well-being and self-worth as less connected to external events and outcomes, whether positive or negative.

(Kelly 2011)

We will be discussing mindfulness further later on in the book.

So, in using the approaches of HR or MTC/IH and PBCC from moment to moment, we need to be aware of, and alert to when we are using personalistic thinking. This would be indicated by our experiencing negative feelings, when all thoughts and feelings relate to our own selves, our own needs, wants and egos, and thinking these thoughts and having these feelings are real. There is a need to learn to stop or let go of this kind of thinking and responding, thereby freeing our thoughts to naturalistic thinking, which is more functionally appropriate and psychologically healthy. In some ways, this personalistic versus naturalistic thinking can be likened to the types of thinking in the mind-brain dichotomy Dan Millman makes earlier in this book. Similarly, Paul Wilson (1987, 26-27) discusses this in relation to meditative/mindful states and also makes the distinction between the quality of mind versus consciousness in a similar way to both personalistic versus naturalistic thinking and Millman's analysis:

> Contrary to popular opinion, the mind is not the custodian of truth and understanding—it is nothing more than the activity of your consciousness. How many times have you thought your 'mind was playing tricks on you', you were 'fooling yourself', or you'd 'convinced yourself' that something or other was true? If your mind was your real master, and not just an activity of your consciousness, why would you suffer so many ego-related problems? Why would your mind delude you into thinking you were sick when all you really wanted was attention; or that you were hungry, when in fact you were sad; that you loved when really you lusted; that you disliked wealthy people when in fact, you envied them? When you control your mind, you have the capacity for greatness. When your mind controls you, you are a slave to your ego and your senses.

Wilson (Ibid.) asserts that meditation teaches you 'how to quiet your mind and, in doing so, elevate your consciousness' and that meditation is a 'reliable way of differentiating between romance and reality.'

In contrast to thinking and processing approaches, we now turn to an approach that disregards these, positing human behaviour as the only phenomena relevant to understanding human nature, and therefore, for our purposes, by implication, the human condition.

Man as Learning Machine

The consequences of an act affect the probability of its occurring again.

Give me a child and I'll shape him into anything.

Education is what survives when what has been learned has been forgotten.

B. F. Skinner

As originating in the works of Ivan Pavlov, Edward Thorndike, John B. Watson and B. F. Skinner, behavioural psychology asserts that it is only through analysis of my external, observable behaviour that we can have insight into what I am and why I do what I do. What goes on in my head and heart is of little, or secondary, scientific value in understanding human nature.

Philosophically and scientifically, this approach regards my internal processes (i.e. thinking and feeling) as a black box, because: (i) they cannot be observed and studied scientifically; (ii) they can be considered as behaviours also, since they underlie and translate into my observable actions.

Am I merely a product of, or constituted in, my myriad learned behaviours over the course of my life time? For example, behaviours that would have been fashioned, or conditioned, through reinforcement contingencies to environmental stimuli, such as reward-punishment, pleasure-pain, or positive-negative experiences.

Are all my actions, feelings, and thoughts linked to (and learnt through) favouring some things (in the extreme leading to compulsions, addictions, etc.), and avoiding others (in the extreme leading to aversions, fears, phobias, etc.)? A burnt hand, being bitten by a dog, an electric shock, being trapped in a lift, getting mugged or attacked, getting bullied or abused, being in a car crash, getting an 'A' grade, getting a medal, getting promoted, getting a pay rise, learning to drive, learning to read, learning to cross the road, falling in love, being hurt by love, making love, smoking, drinking alcohol, taking drugs. I will have learned from all these experiences and will, in future, behave in accordance with those experiences. I will do more of the things that led to a positive experience and avoid altogether or do less of those that led to a negative experience.

But, is it really this simple? Why is it that a racing car driver involved in a serious accident on the track will get back into a car again and race? Stuntmen, like Evel Knievel, perform stunts again and again following serious physical injuries.

Soldiers continue to fight and risk their lives, despite experiencing life-threatening near misses and seeing horrific incidents or injuries. What about romantic love? Why, when we may have been hurt, heartbroken, and traumatised by a relationship breakdown, do we go through the same thing again and again with new partners?

As well as the short-term high, or rush in taking risks that the driver or stuntman gets as the reinforcing reward, there may be longer-term rewards that explain his contradictory behaviour, such as money, fame, or ego. For the soldier, the longer-term reward may be honour, pride, bravery, or even altruism, since a person may get the greatest feeling of reward through helping others.

For the broken-hearted lover, as well as the short-term highs of passion and the feelings associated with falling in love, there are the possibilities of longer-term rewards, such as finding themselves, growing old with someone, having children, finding true love, or avoiding loneliness.

And what of those people addicted to drugs, alcohol, or sex? Clearly their main reinforcement is the short-term reward of the immediate high or buzz, the feeling of escape, the anticipation, novelty, or risk. This may outweigh and cause them to ignore the obvious longer-term consequences or downsides, such as the decay of their finances, health, relationships, employment, or ensuing legal problems.

So what can we learn and understand about suffering, using the behavioural model of man? Suffering is essentially an internal process involving thinking and feelings. As stated earlier, this is regarded as a black box. However, as these internal processes/behaviours translate into externalised, observable behaviours, what kind of behaviours might we observe in someone said to be suffering? These behaviours may include restlessness, inactivity, or hyperactivity, slow or fast bodily movements, not speaking, speaking too much (possibly about the object of their suffering), moaning, crying, brooding, pining, not eating, self-harming, and aggression.

Are these learned behaviours? Are we displaying them because they let others know what our state of mind is and, therefore, we are rewarded through receiving help, sympathy, or comfort, as we may have done throughout our childhood? Is suffering a kind of learned helplessness? If this is the case, then how do we stop suffering? It would appear that behaviourism's answer may be to encourage, through reinforcement and reward, non-suffering type behaviours and actions, such as physical activity, social interaction, laughing, having fun, eating healthily, personal grooming and care, helping others with their problems, getting involved in work and projects, taking up a new interest or hobby. The rewards/benefits felt by the sufferer through these activities may reinforce these positive (learned) behaviours. As external behaviour and (as far as behaviourists think this exists) internal behaviour (i.e. thoughts and feelings) are thought to be correlated, then the former may affect or change the latter. Behaviourism would not make any claims, as such, on which direction the relationship takes, or whether thoughts and feelings (the black box) cause behaviour or vice versa (the chicken and egg scenario), but if the sufferer behaves (and feels) more positively, this is the overriding outcome.

In contrast to limiting understanding of the human condition to only observable learned and conditioned behaviour, the next approach stresses unconscious, psychic processes, which are thought to determine and explain human behaviour and experience.

Psychical Man

Give sorrow words; the grief that does not speak
Whispers the o'er fraught heart, and bids it break.

William Shakespeare, *Macbeth* (1606)

Psychodynamic and psychoanalytic theory (as originated by Sigmund Freud and developed by Melanie Klein, et al.) asserts that essentially I (my personality) am a product of and determined by my unconscious. My moment-by-moment actions, behaviours, thoughts, feelings and emotions; my anxieties and neuroses; my relationship to myself and others are all governed by unconscious wishes, drives, instincts, fantasies, and defences originating in the early, preverbal/primitive mother-child experience.

As a baby, I relied, and was dependent upon, my mother for meeting all my physical and emotional needs: feeding me when hungry; comforting, holding, and reassuring me when frightened or in pain; responding to and sharing in my feelings of joy, contentment, and achievement, etc. I necessarily formed a relationship and bonded with my mother—a relationship underpinned by dependency and attachment.

Since I was unable to speak, and could not distinguish between myself and the world/others, most of my relating and experience was preverbal. These experiences, whether positive or negative (depending on how 'good' a mother I had), remain with me into adulthood and underpin my basic personality, sense of self, and outlook on the world. Because these experiences were preverbal and instinctual prior to intellect and rationalisation, they remain not in my conscious, but buried within my unconscious mind.

My internal representation, or map of the world (i.e. a psychic reality), is constructed and experienced through a number of unconscious, psychic processes that were established in early infancy in my relationship with my mother.

I project onto others bad things, feelings, or parts of myself that I may want to throw out or disown. I introject, or take in, good things, feelings, or parts of others I want to keep and incorporate into my own self. Too much of this splitting, and my personality is in danger of becoming paranoid/schizoid, or narcissistic. If I am able to balance and accept the coexistence of good and bad parts in myself and others, although I will reach what Klein terms the 'depressive position', this is deemed as psychologically and emotionally healthy. Therefore, I can accept, deal, and cope with the possibility and reality of a significant other, myself, and life in general, having both good and bad aspects. Psychoanalytic theory suggests that this idea of good and bad comes from the baby's concept of good breast/bad breast. This stems from a mother's breast sometimes offering the baby milk (good breast) and sometimes not (bad breast); and, therefore, the baby's ability to recognise and accept that the good and bad breasts are one and the same thing, and belong to the same person upon which it relies.

My internal world is not a direct reflection of the external world. Internal objects are phantasies, or fantasised versions of external objects. For example (as alluded to in the Introduction), internal representations of my partner, mother, father, boss, etc. are not real but idealised versions (or phantasies), which are based on my fantasies, desires, wishes, and archetypes (vis-à-vis Jung) of feminine, masculine, leader, etc., which are rooted in childhood, the social psyche, and prehistory.

In relating to others through the process of transference, I also may regard and perceive people as significant others from my past (e.g. my wife as my mother, or my boss as my father). Equally, through projective identification, I may get another person to feel the negative way I feel, since I may not be able to cope with the feeling. I, therefore, unconsciously project this onto someone else in the hope that they will be able to contain the feeling and return it to me in a more handleable or bearable form, in the same way I did as a dependent infant with my mother or father.

How then may we understand suffering from this psychoanalytic model of the human condition?

Essentially, my suffering relates to my emotional life and my relations with myself and others, and may stem largely from my unconscious. My early mother-child emotional development has determined the patterns by which I take in and represent the world and my relationship to it, as well as how I see myself. Depending on my reaching the depressive position of development (i.e. acceptance of reality, of coexistence of both good and bad in the world, in others, and in myself), I could see the world, others, and myself as predominantly bad or as good. I could feel predominantly bitter, angry, anxious, depressed; or accept that others and the world (and myself) are not perfect; that I may not always get what I want; or that things may not always turn out how I'd like them. I may be able to cope and stand on my own two feet, or I may need and depend on others for my emotional well-being and survival, as well as to be able to feel good about myself.

My suffering, in part, may be due to the unrealistic phantasies or idealisations I hold in my unconscious, based on wishes, desires, instincts, fantasies, and archetypes. When the actual object or person does not act in accordance with, or meet my expectations of the phantasy, I may experience fear, distress, anxiety, anger, depression and feel let down.

In my relations with others, part of my failure and subsequent suffering may be in my overly projecting my negative feelings onto them, thereby, seeing them as bad, and thereby, treating them badly and pushing them away. Additionally, through too much projective identification, I may be getting others to feel the negative feelings I feel, again, adversely affecting a relationship. Through too much transference, I may, for example, be regarding and, therefore, relating to a partner as my mother, with all the pressures this can bring to the relationship. If through my early development, I began to see the world as overly or generally bad, I may have had to begin to rely on myself for emotional comfort and developed an over-inflated view of self-worth (i.e. a 'narcissistic' personality). Such a personality requires a high level of maintenance of self-image, shown to others and the world. And in sustaining this, or more so when these endeavours fail, I will experience a degree of suffering, including anger, stress, anxiety, fear of failure, guilt, and depression.

As my need, dependency, and attachment to others and my sense of self were established in my early relationship with my mother and unconsciously underpin my adult relationships, when I lose a cherished partner through divorce, relationship breakdown, bereavement, etc., I may regress to early childhood and suffer deeply. It may feel like losing my mother and, therefore, a part of my self who will feed, protect, comfort, nurture, hold, and value me, and share in my joy and achievements. I may feel anxiety, sadness, fear, rejection, anger, guilt, lost, or deserted. I may become distressed, despondent, and depressed, displaying all the behaviours of a child rejected or deserted by its mother. John Bowlby (as quoted by Josephine Klein 1997), in studying primates and babies, developed theories in the areas of human attachment, loss, separation, and mourning. During early infancy, the baby or primate necessarily becomes attached to its carer (the object). When removed or separated from the carer, the infant/primate displays signs of distress, anxiety, and sometimes anger. If the carer does not ever return, the infant/primate becomes despondent and depressed, and needs to be allowed to mourn the loss if it is to recover and go on to form attachments or relationships with other carers or objects. Neurotic behaviour may be indicated in the subject's 'persistent disbelief that the loss is permanent; a repeated urge to call for, search for, and recover the lost person; prolonged yearning for the lost person; a sense of reproach against the lost person, combined with unremitting self-reproach' (Josephine Klein 1997, 109). So in dealing with suffering relating to loss, mourning and acceptance of the loss underpins healthy recovery and the ability to form future attachments to new objects.

Within the psychoanalytic perspective, as well as referring to people, objects, and object relations, may also refer to things vis-à-vis transitional objects, or objects that substitute, represent, or symbolise people. Therefore, the same processes described above in relation to significant others may also apply to the material world—material or valued possessions and objects. We may form a relationship with these objects and project feelings and fantasies onto them. We may become attached to, need, and depend on them. And crucially, suffer loss of them in the same way as we would a person. We may lose our money, house, job, car, looks, sexual virility, or modern conveniences. We may suffer loss through addiction if we give up cigarettes, alcohol, drugs, gambling, and junk food.

In contrast to a hidden, unconscious and deterministic approach to the human condition, the next approach stresses the conscious, lived experience of being human with all its facets and the primacy of human agency and free will.

Man as Human

'Tis in ourselves that we are thus, or thus. Our bodies are our gardens, to which our wills are gardeners. So that if we will plant nettles or sow lettuce, set hyssop and weed up thyme, supply it with one gender of herbs or distract it with many, either to have it sterile with idleness or manured with industry, why the power and corrigible authority of this lies in our wills.

William Shakespeare, *Othello* (1603-04)

Suit the action to the word, the word to the action.

William Shakespeare, *Hamlet* (1601)

Thus far, we have been looking at scientific and empirical approaches to understanding the human condition and suffering. Humanistic approaches, based philosophically on phenomenology, existentialism, and hermeneutics, focus on the experience and meaning of being human, which they assert is prior to, and of more import than, any scientific ideas of underlying biological, neurological, psychological, behavioural, cognitive, psychoanalytic, and evolutionary determinants of the human condition. After all, it is only in the here and now, the minute-by-minute unfolding of living and human experience in which we can exist, at the confluence of all and any underlying human processes—be they scientific or otherwise.

As a human being, I have a conscious mind. I am fully aware of the way I think, feel, and behave as well as the decisions and choices I make. Those things which are outside of my awareness, or are unconscious, may have little meaning to my immediate, here and now, lived experience. I have intention, free will and agency. I am an authentic individual—a person. I am the author of my own meaning. I produce and use narratives that define, or identify, who I am and my life. I alone can experience my world. I am born alone. I have to live my life—no one else can do this for me. I have to die alone. I am aware that I exist; I live within my own skin.

Whilst these existential features of being human give meaning to and help build my life materially, emotionally, and socially, and give me a self-identity, the very same features underlie my suffering. For when, through life events, such as divorce, relationship breakdowns, bankruptcy, bereavement, or terminal illness, I lose meaning or purpose, control or choice, my identity or my life-narrative, I am confronted by the existential reality of being human and the fragility of my life—of ultimate nothingness and aloneness, my responsibility to make choices, and the ticking away of my time on this earth. Existentialist approaches and therapies highlight that suffering, and existential angst, are part and parcel of being human and part of the human spirit. If I didn't suffer, I wouldn't be human (by implication, I would be some other form of life).

Although this approach paints a fairly grim picture of the human condition, we can see how, through understanding, accepting, and embracing the fragility of our lives, we may be better able to cope with our suffering—in fact, become stronger. We may begin to re-evaluate our lives and look for joy, happiness, and meaning in the non-material world; in everyday social interaction and in the natural world; and most importantly, in the here and now because this is the only one thing we can know and experience for sure.

In overcoming existential suffering, we need firstly to be able to value and love ourselves, accept ourselves and our feelings, be true to ourselves and live authentically and courageously, and not live life according to others' maps, but according to our own. It is only then, that we may truly detach ourselves from the emotional, psychological, social, and material conditions that bind us to others and blind us to ourselves.

The humanistic psychologist, Carl Rogers (1951, 1959) posits in his person-centred and humanistic approach, that we all have an 'organismic self', which has a tendency (and strives naturally) toward growth, realisation (or actualisation), fulfilment, and happiness. Early negative experience with significant others such as parents' conditional love, judgemental-ness, lack of prizing or strokes, congruence, and empathy toward the child can distort, or damage the organismic self, thereby creating a self that is inauthentic and which loses the ability to self-actualise. The resulting grown adult may then have low self-esteem and self-worth, and lack confidence and self-awareness; they may have identity issues, suffer depression, or have an inability to fully experience their true inner self and the world around them. This adult may, therefore, be prone to lacking the personal skills, wisdom, and self-awareness needed in order to tackle their suffering. The person-centred therapist develops a relationship with the client that aims to rectify this damage to the client's sense of self. Through listening, offering unconditional positive regard, prizing, empathising, and not judging, they allow the client to fully experience their feelings, thereby, helping the client to create and value their own internal map in order to reach their full human potential (to self-actualise). The client may then acquire the strength, self-awareness, wisdom, and personal skills to deal more effectively with life events that may cause him or her to suffer.

Another approach that emphasises living authentically and fully in the here and now, the organismic self, and its tendency toward self-actualisation, is that of Fritz Perls' Gestalt therapy. This approach believes that 'personality is comprised of a number of functions—bodily, perceptual, verbal/cognitive—that interrelate closely and exist in relation to the environment' (Parlett & Page 1990, 177).

The organism (the person) needs to interact with the environment in order to obtain and fulfil what it needs to grow and develop to its full potential. Individual needs may be biological, physical, psychological, social, and spiritual. Fulfilling these 'requires full phenomenological awareness, (i.e. recognising and attending to the sensations, feelings and thoughts, which come together as an experience of need)' (Ibid.).

Psychological health and disturbance, therefore, are not mental but organismic, relating to the whole mind-body-spirit system of the organism. The organism needs to be able to respond to, and act upon, the environment in order to maintain balance and equilibrium. When a person is unable, or their ability to do this is impaired, their functioning may be seen to be disturbed.

The theory suggests that we are continually in a process of experiencing gestalts—temporary configurations or imbalances in need(s). A need to get something from the environment—or something of interest that stands out and needs attending to—is seen, or experienced, as the 'figure' (the dominant need at any one time). Everything else in our experience at that time, is being kept in abeyance, and is seen as the 'ground'.

As any given need increases in intensity, we are inclined and mobilised to act and obtain that which we need to satisfy this need from the environment. When this is achieved, balance is restored and this gestalt dissipates, and a new gestalt begins to form.

Gestalt therapy suggests a 'Cycle of Awareness' (Parlett & Page 1990, 178-179) which needs to be gone through successfully within each arising gestalt for healthy functioning.

Stage One: 'Sensing and feeling'—to recognise the dominant need or imbalance, you need to be able to sense and feel it.

Stage Two: 'Becoming aware'—allowing these feelings/sensations into awareness and realising what needs to happen.

Stage Three: 'Mobilising'—beginning to take the initial moves toward acting.

Stage Four: 'Taking action'—fully prepared to take action.

Stage Five: 'Engaging fully'—actually fully engaged with the action (in full flight) physically, mentally, emotionally, and experientially, with full concentration and involvement.

Stage Six: 'In final contact'—engagement reaches its high point, after which action stops and the need dissipates.

Stage Seven: 'Integrating'—taking in fully what has happened, and noticing the positive effects of taking that action, and realising what may need to happen in future as this need arises again.

Stage Eight: 'Letting go'—this is marked by a loss of interest and concentration.

Stage Nine: 'In equilibrium'—no need or imbalance is registered and the person is satisfied. No attention is given to the current gestalt—the person's experience has moved on.

This process of moment-by-moment gestalts arising, evolving, and self-destructing, is seen as the person adjusting creatively and healthily, in the here and now, to their environment in order to meet their biological, physical, psychological, social, and spiritual needs. 'The emerging and receding of different gestalts is a continuous, unending process which, when operating freely, represents successful creative adjustment' (Ibid. 179).

However, psychological disturbances can occur when people are unable to successfully move through the stages of the Cycle of Awareness. Interruptions can occur at any of the stages. They may get stuck or blocked—for example, failing to recognise a need and not allowing feelings and sensations to enter their awareness. Or perhaps, recognising a need or feeling, and failing to mobilise themselves, or once successfully engaging with the environment, failing to let go or hanging onto an experience. A block at any stage may inhibit passing through the full cycle to resolution, leaving the person dissatisfied. Perls called these incomplete gestalts 'unfinished business'.

Many of the problems to do with successfully negotiating gestalts relates to awareness and contact with the environment.

Perls defined three types of awareness (Ibid. 180-181):

(i)   'awareness of self'—a person's direct experience of his or her feelings, emotions, and physical sensations at the time he or she is having them;

(ii) 'awareness of the world'—through the five senses; and

(iii) 'awareness of what's between'—a person's representation of his or her internal world and external reality, including thinking, planning, worrying, remembering, etc. Healthy functioning occurs when the person accurately represents their internal and external reality by integrating the two in creative adjustment.

Parlett and Page (1990, 180) describe contact as occurring:

> When the organism is fully in touch with the environment and engaging with it, there is full sensory awareness and activation of the motoric system, as well as an accompanying internal feeling state. In everyday language we refer to people being 'in touch', they are 'all there'. In dysfunction, this ability to be present and in touch is lost: the differentiation of the individual's experience of himself from his experience of the environment (the 'contact boundary') is distorted, leading to an interruption of contact.

Parlett and Page (Ibid.) go onto suggest that because dysfunctioning people cannot always know (or experience) the difference between themselves (the self) and their environment (the not-self) (i.e. what is theirs and what is outside of themselves or belonging to the environment or others) they may display a number of disturbances at the contact boundary.

They may inadvertently take in (introject) from the environment and become responsible for messages, beliefs, and feelings that they themselves do not hold or feel, but begin to believe in and experience as their own ('I am no good', 'I am ugly', 'I am a failure', etc.).

They may project onto the environment or others their own feelings, beliefs, and thoughts, thereby locating the causation (and responsibility) for these in external objects or others, rather than taking responsibility for their own feelings (perhaps blaming the latter). This results in thoughts such as 'You make me so angry' (when you are angry with yourself); 'You don't love me' (when it's perhaps you that doesn't love her); or 'I don't trust him' (when it's yourself that you cannot trust).

Because they cannot engage with their environment (perhaps it is seen as too dangerous) and meet their needs successfully in this way, they may (through retroflection) self-manipulate, or do things to themselves to meet these needs. For example, if they are angry with someone or something in the environment, they harbour aggressive impulses and are then unable to express these to someone else. They may physically harm themselves; or, if they need, but are unable to obtain affection from the environment or others, they may physically hug themselves, comfort, or reward themselves in other ways.

Because they cannot differentiate between themselves and their environment or others (confluence), they may be avoiding separateness. The contact boundary weakens, with them not knowing where they and their environment begin and end. They are unable to make good contact with others, but at the same time cannot withdraw from them. They may end up acquiescing with others, merging with the crowd, avoiding conflict and failing to differentiate their own needs.

When there are persistent interruptions like these, in the cycle of awareness, an accumulation of uncompleted gestalts (unfinished business) occur, leaving the person in a constantly unfulfilled state. And even though they still have a variety of needs; they may continue to fulfil them in these dysfunctional ways. The person may

> develop fixed patterns of adapting, getting by, or manipulating, which are so habitual and taken for granted that they are not easily accessible to the person's present awareness. They can be thought of as fixed gestalts, with the person's cycles of experience being interrupted in a similar way over and over again, leading to stereotyped reactions and behaviours. The person does not realise that she has a choice—that she does not need to be stuck with an obsolete response.
>
> (Ibid. 182)

> Automatic patterns of thinking, moving, feeling or holding herself posturally—many of them self-damaging or self-limiting—remain in existence because the person keeps trying to actualise her self-image rather than her actual self, and to grasp that the two are not identical means unsettling the status quo.
>
> (Ibid. 183)

We can see through the Gestalt approach that people may continue to suffer, by not allowing for their own organismic (moment-by-moment) biological, physical, psychological, social, and spiritual needs and feelings to come into full awareness in the here and now. And by not meeting these needs through fully engaging (vis-à-vis full contact) with their environment or others—mobilising themselves, taking action, being fully engaged with their environment and themselves, or integrating their experience, thereby learning/growing and letting go of experiences and moving on. In other words, they become stuck in fixed (or unfinished) gestalts (or negative ways of being or experiencing), which are never fully resolved and dissipated, thereby leaving hanging, unfinished business.

Through being unable to differentiate between (and owning) their own self and the not-self (the environment), they may be open to feelings, thoughts, and beliefs about themselves that are not their own, but those of others. They may be disowning, displacing (or projecting) their feelings, thoughts and beliefs onto others, thereby absolving responsibility and denying individual choice. If they do not fully engage and obtain things (in a healthy way) from their environment, which meet their needs, they may resort to self-manipulation and dysfunctional thoughts, beliefs, and behaviours to meet these needs. If they are unable to either engage with, or withdraw from the environment, and are, therefore, unable to achieve separateness, they may lose themselves, their identity, free will, choice, and autonomy by merging in with others, meeting others' needs, and denying their own.

THE GOD WORLD

Spiritual Man

When you see, let there be no seer or seen; when you hear, let there be no hearer or heard; when you think, let there be no thinker or thought.

Zen Master Foyan

(Cleary, *Zen Essence: The Science of Freedom*, 89)

Let go of all your previous imaginings, opinions, interpretations, worldly knowledge, intellectualism, egoism, and competitiveness; become like a dead tree, like cold ashes. When you reach the point where feelings are ended, views are gone, and your mind is clean and naked, you open up to Zen realisation.

Zen Master Yuanwu

(Ibid. 59)

Good and bad come from your own mind. But what do you call your own mind, apart from your actions and thoughts? Where does your own mind come from? If you really know where your own mind comes from, boundless obstacles caused by your own actions will be cleared all at once.

Zen master Dahui

(Ibid. 108)

Although I have a physical, biological, and psychological dimension, am I not more than this? Do I also have a soul or spirit, energy, a spark, a force of life that is me and links me to matter, the natural world and the metaphysical—that part of me that is beyond body, thought, emotion and language? Is there not a part of me that is intangible, without boundary, and indefinable? I may experience this part of me when I watch a beautiful sunset, read a moving poem, listen to music, or look at a painting. Something may touch me or resonate deep down during these experiences. Psychologists have called these experiences 'peak experiences' and are defined when in a moment, some deeper truth and understanding is revealed to us about the world, or an epiphany occurs and we feel wonder, awe, and elation.

The approach taken by religion, spiritualism and mysticism suggests that there is a higher, transpersonal and transcendental dimension to human experience, linked to higher forces or intelligences e.g. God, Tao, Yin-Yang, Buddha, Krishna, and Karma, which have their own nature, energy, and dynamic; their own unfolding. In the West, these approaches may be linked, for example, to Christianity, Judaism, and Paganism. In the East, they may be linked to Buddhism, Zen, Taoism, Hinduism, and Yoga; which assert that there is a higher self beyond the smaller self. This is beyond ego, intellect, and the rational mind, and beyond everyday feelings, emotions, and actions, in fact, even beyond the material world. All of these are deemed to be the causes of human bondage and, therefore, suffering. The self may be located in and attained by reaching higher states of being known as nirvana, enlightenment, dharma, Buddha-nature, Krishna, or transcendental consciousness. Central to these Eastern philosophies is control of the mind. In her study of Eastern yoga and self-realisation, Josephine Ransom (1936, 43-44), elegantly wrote (and it is worth quoting fully):

> In control or direction of the mind lies the crux of the whole ideal of yoga. The mind is a sort of critical turning point in one's human career. It has been the tireless watcher of the endless changes that go on all about it. It has driven the emotions to all their constant clamour for satisfaction. It has been the perceiver of the ceaseless procession of events and has clung to each as it passed in the hope of finding something permanent. To its pain the momentary set of events melts away and leaves it desolate, and at the same time anxious to find the next thing to which to cling. Thus, the mind has changed with the changing, and identified itself with the moment. 'Hinder this game,' Patanjali advised, 'hinder the modifications of this thinking principle in you. Stop all this, and when you do you will know yourself as the "Seer"—the "seer of the essence of things."' (Sri Krishna, Bhagavad Gita)

Eastern yogas, based on the Hindu Vedas, link suffering to emotional, psychological, and bodily attachment (i.e. birth and death); to the material world; to desire and striving in relation to satisfying the ego and the senses; to the belief that we are in control through our acting on the world; to our dualistic thinking (desire and hate, happiness and distress, good and bad). Once we attach ourselves to an outcome or result, whether positive or negative, we become attached to the resulting emotions (the cause of bondage). Therefore, just to act is sufficient, without aligning outcomes to ourselves. As Lord Krishna advises Arjuna in the Bhagavad Gita:

> One who is attached to the result of his work is also the cause of the action. Thus he is the enjoyer or sufferer of the result of such actions.
>
> **Prabhupada** 1972, 37

The yogas also believe that contemplation of sense-objects leads to attachment for them; from this attachment lust, pleasure, and desire arise and from these, anger and:

> From anger, delusion arises, and from delusion bewilderment of memory. When memory is bewildered, intelligence is lost, and when intelligence is lost, one falls down again into the material pool.
>
> Ibid. 42

Therefore, control of the senses and freedom from both attachment and aversion may relieve us of our suffering and bondage. The Vedas posit a complete model of the human condition; likening the body to a chariot driven by five horses:

> The horses are the five sense organs—the tongue, eyes, ears, nose and skin. The reins are the mind, the driver is the intelligence, and the passenger is the spirit soul. One must, with the help of intelligence, control the mind and senses otherwise they will pull one, like wild horses, toward ruination
>
> Ibid. XI

And it is through the mechanical means of practicing yoga (including meditation), that one can control the mind.

Spiritual or transpersonal approaches suggest that, in effect, we create our own suffering. We act unwittingly in an automatic and unthinking way in accordance with, and to satisfy, our conditioned and delusional minds, desires, needs, wants, and emotions. And these often can be based on ego, greed, avarice, power, jealousy, self-interest, fear, etc. Although these actions may initially bring about emotional reward, they may also create attachments, and subsequently, lead to negative emotions, unhappiness, and suffering, especially when the objects of our actions are lost to, or become unfulfilling for us.

Although in the complex modern world, it is difficult to fully detach emotionally and psychologically from the material world and relationships (i.e. become an ascetic, a hermit, or a monk), the spiritual approach teaches us to stand back and think about the motives for, and origins of, our actions and thoughts. Are they based on self-interest (i.e. ego), anger, jealousy, fear, greed, dualistic thinking (e.g. good-bad, loss-gain, winner-loser, perpetrator-victim, happiness-sadness, success-failure, cause-effect), or the need for control? If, so, then we must stop or modify these actions and thoughts, because these constitute (and lead to) our suffering.

Anxiety, depression, stress and other mental health problems often relate to the way we think, our beliefs and attitudes about ourselves, others and the world in general. This may lead to our dwelling on (or obsessing), fearing, or worrying about things, including our self-worth, the past, present, or future. Increasingly, helping people to change the way they think and react (emotionally and behaviourally) to events in the fields of counselling, psychotherapy, clinical psychology and psychiatry, the theory and practice of Mindfulness (as discussed earlier), originating in Zen Buddhist psychology and meditation, has been applied (Kabat-Zinn 2009; Shapiro et al. 2006; Segal et al. 2002; Bishop et al. 2004; Christopher & Maris 2010).

Based on Buddhism's views that we cannot control the world, our past or the future, that our moment-to-moment thinking and feeling may be reactive/reflexive, automatic, egotistic, reflecting our own patterns/gestalts and projections, that we cannot be defined by our thoughts and feelings, as unitary/unified monotheistic selves. Mindfulness practice teaches us to merely observe our moment-to-moment experiences (i.e. our thoughts, feelings, and sensations) as these arise, and accept them freely, with equanimity, curiosity, and without judgement or secondary appraisal (vis-à-vis non-reactivity). This focus on, and attention to, the present may be achieved through our cultivating the capacities for non-distraction, letting-go/non-elaboration of thoughts, attention switching and self-regulating attention on moment-to-moment experience (Aggs & Bambling 2010). In this way we may be able to disidentify and decentre ourselves from our negative internal dialogues, states, and perspectives as these arise (Christopher & Maris 2010, 121); seeing these as just that and not as what define, reflect, or determine our selves.

It can be noted that these spiritual approaches based on Mindfulness (as well as the MTC/IH/PBCC and personal thinking discussed earlier) appear to contradict those of Rogers and Gestalt—the organismic/self-actualisation approaches. The former stresses the being aware of, but letting go of personalistic thoughts, feelings, and emotions in the present moment, because these are illusory. The latter stresses being aware of and acknowledging these by being congruent and truthful about what you are experiencing, and acting on them, venting, and completing them (e.g. gestalts) in the belief these are authentic and constitute and reflect the needs of the real/organismic self.

Perhaps the former approaches are aligned to Eastern philosophies, which eschew the idea of control and action (believing in fate and other controlling forces in the universe) and the concept of the individual. These philosophies are instead more focused on the whole, the group, the transpersonal, whereas, the latter approaches may be aligned to Western philosophies, which do recognise the existence and value of the essential individual and their ability to act on and change the world. They are situated within a milieu of self-responsibility, determinism, positivism, rationalism, and science with a belief in cause and effect.

THE SOCIAL WORLD

Man as Social Construction

What's in a name? That which we call a rose
By any other name would smell as sweet.
William Shakespeare, *Romeo and Juliet* (1595)

I am an individual, with my own personality and psychology, my own identity and self. I live within my own skin. I have my own memories, my own history, life story, or narrative.

But can any of these things mean anything outside of the language I use, or the culture and social world I inhabit? Am I not a product of, and constituted in, language, culture, and the social world? Am I not able to change who I am, my identity? Are not the arrays and repertoires, or discourses, of thoughts, beliefs, and attitudes I have; the actions I take, my behaviours and emotions; my life narrative(s), the identities I take on, all constructed and defined by the social, linguistic, and cultural world? Does language and culture reflect and help us to express our true human inner selves and experience? Or are our true human inner selves and experience mere reflections or expressions of, and constituted in, language and culture itself?

As outlined in the Introduction, the postmodern, post-structuralist or constructionist approach to the human condition would argue that there is no core, stable essence to the individual. The individual is merely the 'subject of language' (Redman 2000), constructed by and constituted in the I, me, and you, as used in language, subjectified (as posited by Michel Foucault) by social and institutional discourses and practices (e.g. wife, husband, student, teacher, teenager, deviant, criminal, patient, or addict).

However, the question this postmodernist approach does raise is: If there is nothing under the skin, why, then, do we feel like individual selves, therefore, feel emotional and psychological pain and behave in psychologically and organismically unhealthy/dysfunctional ways, with some of us developing emotional, psychological, and behavioural problems?

Are we merely socially and culturally enacting, or acting out, suffering as the victim, depressed, anxious, or stressed person, bereaved person, mentally ill person, loner, madman, hysterical woman, etc., in order that we can tacitly gain sympathy, help, support, social advantage, or merely find a way out of dealing with the stresses, strains, and problems that assail us in our everyday living, or having to make choices?

If this line of argument were to be true, then it would follow that in order to stop my suffering, I would need to take on and inhabit a more positive subjective construct, identity, or narrative such as that of a survivor, or a person who is strong, confident, wise, intelligent, stable, optimistic, happy, contented, a person who is a winner, a glass half-full person, someone who enjoys their own company, and is socially popular. And in doing this, my thoughts, attitudes, beliefs, and behaviours would change accordingly.

As a member of a society, I have a sociopolitical identity as produced by social institutions, a personhood or rather, multiple-personhoods/social identities. For example, a legal personality (McFarquhar 2000) which inheres legal and ethical rights, statuses, responsibilities, attributes, and duties (e.g. I am a manager, teacher, partner, citizen, voter, taxpayer, father, son, house owner, employee, patient, divorcee, husband, Sikh of Indian nationality or ethnicity, heterosexual of male gender, landlord or tenant). My multiple personhoods give me the feeling of being a subject. But this subject has been produced through subjectification by social institutions, such as marriage, the family, the education system, the law, medicine, and religion. How much is this subject a part of me and my self, and how much a mere social identity and construct? Are my actions my own, or merely those of my social self (or selves)? In which case, is there any part of me that is not socially determined or controlled?

Marcel Mauss (1938), the sociologist/social anthropologist, asserts that notions of the person, self, subject, and consciousness are mere 'internalisations and categories of the mind', produced through historical developments and phenomena, such as Rome (citizenship, legal status), Christianity and the Reformation (moral existence, introspection, prayer, self-consciousness, self-scrutiny, self-regulation of conduct, self-examination of conscience), the 'Protestant work ethic' (Max Weber 1904/05), and the 'cult of the individual' (Emile Durkheim 1858-1917).

Additionally, Mauss asserts that even our bodies are socially regulated/determined through 'techniques of the body'. And he provides a 'catalogue of the ways in which social conventions, physical techniques, and their forms of training and practice, organise activities and abilities that we tend to regard as natural, such as walking, spitting, sleeping, and so forth' (du Gay 2000).

Mauss draws a distinction between the individual, the person, and the subject. The individual being the unstructured raw, human biological and psychological material; the person being a definite complex of statuses and attributes enabling one to conduct oneself socially, with the subject being the (historically/institutionally acquired) internalised sense of self and personhood. Mauss contests that we inadvertently equate person, subject, and consciousness with self; that there is, in fact, no actual, essential, self!

How can this sociolinguistic-cultural perspective help to explain my suffering? These analyses suggest that apart from my raw physiological and psychological material, I am but a myriad of multiple social identities, personas, roles or selves, each determining my being and behaviour within their respective contexts and social milieu.

However, I come to believe that I am a single, stable and enduring subject, an individual, a real self with a real conscience, existing completely within my own skin. Therefore, as well as being linked in part to underlying human and evolutionary physiological processes, my suffering may also stem from my belief, stake in, and attachment to, this self and my often conflicting and demanding multiple personas or roles. Indeed, these social personas may actually determine how I should suffer (i.e. the attitudes and behaviours I should adopt). For example, as well as the physiological and psychological effects of separation and loss that divorce causes: with the role/identity of 'divorcee' or 'separated', I may believe myself, as a subject or individual, to be disintegrating or dissolving. Or, I may consider myself a failure that is to blame. I may become overly introspective, or self-scrutinising, examining my conscience. I may be grieving. With considerable stress and variable success, I have to take on, or adopt, new personas, changing from married to separated or divorced; from a homeowner to a tenant; from full-time father to parent with contact, or a distant parent. Each new persona comes with their particular and prescribed social attitudes and behaviours. Other examples of personas we can take on or inhabit are bereaved, widower, redundant, unemployed, retired, pensioner, criminal, deviant, mentally ill, mad, disabled, etc.

This anti-essentialist/postmodern approach to the human condition explains how we are constructed by, and constituted in, language, culture and discursive practices; and how we are merely subjects inhabiting multiple personas with no real, cohesive, essential self. However, an approach, touched upon earlier, that acknowledges the determining power of language, society, and culture for identity, but seeks to overcome this and give some agency and humanity to the individual, is that of Existentialism. Colin Wilson (*The Outsider*) points out how we come to believe, through delusion, in our socially constructed identities, but how, if we see through these, we may find our true humanities. He quotes William Blake:

> Each man is in his spectre's power
> Until the arrival of that hour
> When his humanity awakes
> And casts his spectre into the lake.

Blake's 'spectre' is the dead, conscious part of man that he mistakes for himself—the personality, the habits, the identity. 'Man is not of fixed or enduring form,' Steppenwolf realised in a moment of insight. But when man is in 'his spectre's power' (and most of us are, every day), he sees himself and the whole world as of 'fixed and enduring form' (Wilson 1978, 251).

In being able to look at ourselves existentially from the outside, Wilson (1978, 280) cites one of George Gurdjieff's four states of consciousness: self-remembering, which suggests that 'we identify ourselves with our personalities; our identities are like the pane of a window against which we are pressed so tightly that we cannot feel our separateness from it. Self-remembering is like standing back, so you can see yourself (the window-pane) and the outside world, distinct from you.' Gurdjieff further suggests (Ibid. 282-283) how we are attached and locked into our identities and suffering through our attachment with our worlds:

> [Man] is attached to everything in his life; attached to his imagination, attached to his stupidity, attached even to his suffering—possibly to his suffering more than anything else. He must free himself from attachment. Attachment to things, identification with things keeps alive a thousand 'I's' in a man. These 'I's' must die in order that the big I may be born.

My suffering, seen from this perspective, may lay in my feeling, or realisation, that I am lost without my social identities and personas—that there is indeed an inner me, an existential self that I have to face and come to terms with. T.S Elliot, in his poem *The*

Hollow Men (1925), highlights the meaninglessness, emptiness, and impotency of this existential self and the human condition:

> We are the hollow men
> We are the stuffed men
> Leaning together
> Headpiece filled with straw. Alas!
> Our dried voices, when
> We whisper together
> Are quiet and meaningless
> As wind in dry grass
> Or rats' feet over broken glass
> In our dry cellar.

However, as Gurdjieff and Blake suggest, in facing and accepting my existential self, devoid of my socially constructed selves and personas, and the suffering this may entail, I may find a truer humanity, begin to live more authentically and strive to find and create a deeper meaning to my life.

THE REAL WORLD

Real Man

Fear not what is not real, never was, and never will be. What is real always was and cannot be destroyed.

Bhagavad Gita

Repetition is the reality and the seriousness of life.

Soren Kierkegaard

Reality is merely an illusion, albeit a very persistent one.

Albert Einstein

Although I may be a product of, and constituted in, my biology, brain chemistry, psychology, the sociolinguistic and cultural context I live in; and I (or reality itself) may be real/essential, imagined, or constructed, I still, nonetheless, inhabit an a priori real world. This is external to me, with its states of affairs, situations and events, with real effects and consequences, which can lead to my suffering.

For example, if, as a plaintiff, I am found guilty of a crime, I may be arrested and imprisoned, and thus would become a criminal. If my employer makes me redundant, I will become unemployed. If, as a homeowner, I am unable to pay my mortgage to the lender, or as a tenant, to the landlord, I may become bankrupt or homeless, and, therefore, unable to support my family. If my wife divorces me or dies, I will become single or separated, or a divorcee or widower, and will have to rebuild my life again. If, as a student, my tutor consistently gives me low scores, I may fail my exams and not get into university. Natural disasters, the economy, racism, social, legal, and political policy may affect my life chances as a citizen. If I am drafted to join the army and become a soldier, I will have to be prepared to fight in wars, kill others, and be killed myself.

The approach of Realism (Smith 1998, 297-307) posits that reality is not—as has been conventionally contested—constituted in, or limited to, either: (a) the empirical/experiential world; or (b) imaginative constructs (i.e. idealism). Reality is to be found in real objects and structures in the world, which have deep, intrinsic, underlying, and enduring properties and contingent (or necessary) relationships. These have the capacity and power to act in certain ways by virtue of these properties (e.g. tutor-student, landlord-tenant, employer-employee, husband-wife, doctor-patient, state-citizen, capital-labour, etc.). It is these real world objects and structures that pre-exist the objects of empirical science, and indeed, are what the latter's studies are based upon. Without them there would be no objects for empirical science to study! It is because of the realness of these objects or structures, that Roy Bhasker (1979, 1986 & 1991) (in Smith, Ibid.) asserts in his *Critical Realism*, that the approach of natural sciences (naturalism) can, and should, be used to study these objects or structures, but, using an open, rather than closed, systems approach—since this recognises complexity and acknowledges a lack of predictability, but still produces good and valid explanations.

Therefore, is it enough, or sufficient, to locate the human condition, reality, and human suffering and its remedies in the workings of the human mind, or in its psychology, biology, brain chemistry, consciousness and human behaviour; or, in the socially constructed cultural-linguistic and discursive world?

What about the external world of events, situations, relations, structures, and agency, and of dealing and interacting with reality as it both viscerally and practically impacts upon us, as we impact upon it?

As well as altering my mind, my brain chemistry, and my behaviour in order to succeed in reducing my suffering, I also have to be able to change the world (my reality, the conditions of my existence) socio-economically, culturally, legally, and politically (e.g. personal relationships, employment, income, housing, health, education, political activity, and representation). Reality may be situated in real world objects, structures, and relations, which have real consequences for people. It may be these that underlie and impact on any examination of the human condition and suffering. To remedy an individual's suffering, therefore, may require changing not only his or her mind, brain, and behaviour, but also the real social objects, structures, and relations in his or her external world.

Book Review

Book Website: www.iqubalbirdi.com

What am I? And Why Do I Suffer?

An Anatomy of the Human Condition: Models of Man and Suffering

how we might alleviate our own suffering by using the principles and strategies suggested by the models.

Birdi was inspired to write this book through his own suffering and it is clear that he has a deep and broad understanding of the subject.

The material is well researched and written in a way that would appeal to the academic, any practitioner concerned with psychological health and well-being, or any interested layperson. It is erudite, lucid and, while accessible to such a variety of potential readers, in no way superficial or condescending. I found it deeply engaging from the first page, recognising that it addressed so many of the questions I had pondered for many years. Here those questions have been explored through many perspectives and brought together in a comprehensive, learned, logical and cohesive way.

For those who wish to research these areas further, or delve into the depths of a particular model or models, or simply use the text for self-exploration and understanding, self-help or discussion, this book is an excellent starting point as it gives a beautifully synthesised description of each model which helps to increase our understanding of the phenomena of what it means to be human, and of our suffering.

I would, recommend this book as an excellent resource to anyone who wants to understand themselves, who they are, what they are and why they suffer. Understanding goes some way towards self-empowerment and healing while the suggested principles for everyday

CONCLUSION

I am an infinitesimally small entity, both biologically and physically. I am set within space and time, constituted within, and inseparable from, the physical universe and nature, as is all matter.

At one level of my being, I am still animal, primitive and evolutionary with basic innate preverbal instincts and drives. I possess an innate social/collective unconscious psyche, spanning the lived experience of humanity with innate cognitive processes and schema relating to memory, knowledge, and language acquisition, learning, problem solving, and intelligence. My brain chemistry can dictate and underlie all my evolutionary behaviours, feelings, and emotions, and also determine my personality. My behaviours may simply be conditioned responses, through positive/negative reinforcement contingencies, to stimuli that I experience in my environment—I learn to be the way I am.

However, I am also a person with an identity, able to attach meaning and purpose to my existence through language, culture, and social practices, as well as through my individual experiences and life narratives, and through the knowledge I acquire. I may also have an innate, organismic propensity to reach my human potential, to self-actualise.

I am also rational in that my thoughts and beliefs about events, myself, and the world may dictate my feelings and, therefore, my behaviours and actions.

Existentially, I am aware. I am reflexive and conscious of my essential mortality and aloneness in the world and the apparent absurdity, futility, and meaninglessness of existence. Therefore, the need for living with true meaning, authenticity, connectivity, and purpose becomes even more of an important goal for which to strive.

As I am a product of a sociolinguistic-cultural world, and necessarily inhabit and exist within this, a significant part of my sense of self, identity, and personhood is constructed by, constituted in, and defined by this world, for example, through language, socially constructed discourses, subject positions, narratives, and personas, as well as subjectification through sociocultural and institutionally discursive practices.

I have a spiritual or transpersonal dimension which negates the need for a self or ego; hence, my sense of being able to control events in the world may be illusory, as may my conditioned thoughts linked to self-interest, value judgements, desires, and attachments to sense objects in the material world.

Whatever I am, I am still connected socioeconomically and politically to the real world. I am connected to social and institutional structures and relationships (e.g. the law, education, housing, welfare, health, citizenship, and employment), which all impact upon my everyday living, and, therefore, dictate what I can and cannot do, what I am entitled to, my level of control and power, and my life chances.

My suffering, then, may be seen to be located within, and constituted by, these different levels of the person, of being and of experiencing. And therefore, my level of suffering may be linked to a number of biopsychosocial factors and capacities.

My ability to change my brain chemistry and cognitive functioning, personality, unconscious drives, conflicts and projections, behavioural conditioning and social learning, thought patterns, attitudes and beliefs about myself and the world. My ability to create meaning and purpose, to re-create/re-define, more positively, my identity, position, situation and life-narrative through the social, linguistic, and cultural discourses and constructs available to me. My ability to live authentically and courageously in light of my existential awareness, conditions and connectivity to others. My ability to change my material living conditions and life chances through the means of acting on and through the necessarily real, sociopolitical and cultural institutions, structures, and relations.

On a spiritual/transpersonal level, as posited by Buddhism and the approach of Mindfulness, my suffering may be linked to my self, my ego, my emotions, my patterns of judgemental, or personalised, dichotomous thinking, my attachment to material/sense objects and relations in the world, as well as birth and death; my ability to live in, enjoy, and experience the here and now, as opposed to living in the past and future; my ability to realise and accept that my sense of controlling events in the world may be illusory; that reality is not fixed but continuously changing and unfolding, from moment to moment—requiring me to allow for and change with this.

The human condition, human nature, consciousness, experience, and behaviour, emotional and psychological distress, and suffering are produced by, and constituted in, different interacting levels or dimensions of the person: physical, biological, neurological, neurochemical, evolutionary, psychological, personality, sociocultural and sociolinguistic, existential, and spiritual (the schematic in Appendix A represents and models this view).

Therefore, it follows that in order to reduce the experience of emotional and psychological distress and suffering, interventions may be made at any or many levels of the person or human experience. Although interventions may be made by professionals (e.g. GPs, psychologists, psychiatrists, and counsellors) in helping us to cope with and/or reduce emotional and psychological suffering, there are things we can do to help ourselves, too. In looking back at, and referring to, the discussions and analyses offered in this book, we may elicit certain principles or approaches we may try to adopt and incorporate into our everyday living.

Improving Emotional and Psychological Well-Being and Reducing Suffering: Principles for Everyday Living

1. Connectedness to, and relationship with, the physical universe, the natural world, and others:

When you think of being alone, the magnitude of your self, your ego, your problems, your suffering, your fear of life and death, know that you are one very small part of the universe. As well, you are necessarily connected to this, through sharing the same matter and energy, which cannot be created or destroyed. Therefore, you are connected to both the physical and natural world and everything and everyone else in it. Buddhism teaches us that all phenomena in the world, including humans, are interconnected and interdependent—we are not separate, individual entities, with separate, inherent realities. Instead, we rely on each other for our survival; and compassion is our true nature. With this awareness, we need increasingly, to make the 'We' more real than the 'I', and be more guarded against using the 'my', 'mine', or 'me'.

2. Brain, body and behaviour—positive emotional states:

Although increasing the feel-good chemicals in your brain can be done in negative ways (e.g. misusing food, alcohol, drugs, gambling, sex, or risk taking), it can also be achieved through more positive means, such as exercising, meditation, yoga, relaxation, laughing more, eating a healthy diet, and engaging in positive social and intimate relationships, all of which give a sense of connectedness and belonging. As well, partaking in learning, experiencing new and novel things, and being creative can also give a sense of excitement, joy, fulfilment, and self-efficacy. Helping others, or doing kind acts toward others, gives a sense of altruism and feels rewarding.

Other positive means could be reviewing your day and thinking what has made you happy and what went well, or recalling and thinking about happy or positive moments in your life. Increasing your exposure to positive external and internal events and stimuli creates positive emotional states and, therefore, positive feelings, as well as positive thinking and behaviour.

3. Thinking, feeling and behaving—rational and natural thinking:

If you are feeling anxious, fearful, worried, or depressed, become aware of, recognise, and reflect on: (i) What event has just occurred, that triggered these feelings? (ii) What are your thoughts, beliefs, and assumptions about the event? Question these—are they rational? What is the evidence for these thoughts/beliefs / assumptions? Are they justified? (iii) What other, more positive and rational ways could you think about the event? Your thoughts may relate to awfulising, magnifying, or over-generalising. You may be abstracting things selectively about the event. Your thinking may be dichotomous (i.e. all or nothing). (iv) Note how re-conceptualising the event and changing your thoughts, beliefs, and assumptions, makes you feel now, and what positive, rather than negative, behaviours and actions you may now undertake.

Learn to recognise all thoughts that relate to you personally or are about you (i.e. personal thinking). Learn to let these thoughts come and go out of your awareness, without attending or responding to them. In other words, detach yourself from them, because it is misuse/overuse of this type of thinking that causes the most emotional distress. You can recognise personal thinking when you experience and choose to dwell, or spend effort on negative, unsettling, painful emotions, feelings, and memories; or when your thoughts involve worrying; thinking ambivalently, judgementally, obsessively, angrily, egoistically; or indulging in perfectionist thinking; or thinking that self-esteem has to be earned. Instead, learn to trust your naturalistic thinking—the innate, generic, intelligent, automatic/human default thinking with which you were born. This default surfaces automatically when your mind quiets or clears—when you stop trying to think. Naturalistic thinking requires no conscious effort and no stress. It produces all the positive psychological experiences for your mental health and is automatically responsive to the moment by providing you with sensory data appropriate to your immediate needs and goals.

4. Changing behaviour

Behaving and acting in positive ways reinforces the positive behaviour, the associated positive thoughts and feelings of the behaviour, and the positive sense of self, self-efficacy, self-worth, and reward. Behaving and acting in negative ways reinforces the negative behaviour, the associated negative thoughts and feelings of the behaviour, and the negative sense of self, self-efficacy, self-worth, and negative reward.

For example, giving a successful public presentation that was previously something you feared will reinforce your ability to give public presentations in future. From that experience will come associated positive thoughts and feelings of giving a public presentation along with a positive sense of self, self-efficacy, self-worth, and reward. Not giving the feared public presentation will reinforce your inability and fear in giving public presentations in future. From this will come associated negative thoughts and feelings in not giving a public presentation (e.g. *Phew! I'm glad I didn't do that, as I would have been a wreck. I would have made a mess of it and people would have laughed at me.*), along with a negative sense of self, self-efficacy, self-worth (e.g. *I'm no good. I'm hopeless at giving public presentations.*), and negative reward (e.g. *Phew! I've saved myself a lot of embarrassment by not giving that presentation. It's safer for me to continue to avoid doing presentations in future.*).

5.   Relations with yourself, others, and the world:

Learn to be aware of what emotions and feelings are yours, and own them (e.g. anger, fear, hostility, rejection, mistrust, being unloved, and uncared for). Do not project or transfer these onto others (or onto external objects), making them responsible for what you are feeling. Do not make it appear it is they who have these feelings and emotions toward you (e.g. they are angry at you, frightening, hostile toward you, rejecting and mistrusting of you, or it is they who do not love you, and are uncaring toward you).

Learn to accept the possibility and reality that both good and bad aspects, can co-exist, side-by-side in yourself, others, and in the world. Do not reject, disown, or split these to suit your own needs and fantasies, or your own sense of security and self-worth. Learn to accept that you, others, and the world are not perfect; that you may not always get what you want; that things may not always turn out how you would like them. Know that you are able to cope and stand on your own two feet; you do not need or depend on others for your emotional well-being and survival, or to feel good about yourself.

In forming attachments to others and objects in the world, allow for mourning and acceptance of loss in order to allow healthy recovery and the ability to form future attachments to new objects or people.

Learn to balance the needs, urges, drives, and desires of your ego with the positive norms and values of your own moral conscience, as well as those of society.

6.   Experiencing the self in the here and now:

You are only able to experience yourself and the world in the here and now. Develop self awareness of how you are feeling in the present. Allow yourself to sense, experience, and accept feelings, emotions, and thoughts, whether positive or negative, without judgement, guilt, and self-reprisals. Then let go of these. This is you in this moment, and you are allowed to experience fully and honestly whatever is happening internally for you. This is a natural process and to block it, may impede resolution, personal growth, development, and learning. Through this way of being you may be able to discover, get in touch with, and accept, your true and authentic self without hidden, and previously conditioned, distortions of any kind, as well as increase your sense of self-worth and self-estcem.

Learn to accurately sense, perceive, and engage with what is happening internally for you and what is happening in your environment. Healthy functioning in meeting your needs (i.e. gestalts) occurs when you accurately represent your internal and external reality and integrate the two in creative adjustment. Disturbances in this healthy process can occur when you are unable to differentiate, or separate, yourself from your environment and between what belongs to you and what belongs to the environment. You may project your own feelings, emotions, thoughts, and beliefs onto others, making them responsible for these. You may take in feelings, emotions, thoughts, and beliefs of others, making yourself responsible for these. To avoid separation and/or conflict, you may merge with and disappear into the environment, others, the crowd—thereby acquiescing with others and fail to differentiate yourself and your own needs.

Successful resolution of meeting your needs in this way through accurately experiencing and representing yourself and the environment, will lead to your moving on (i.e. completed or dissipated gestalts). Unsuccessful resolution—through disturbances in this process—will lead to unfinished business (i.e. fixed gestalts).

7. Existential awareness and acceptance, living meaningfully and authentically:

We are conscious, sentient beings, but often we may avoid the existential reality and angst that we will eventually and inevitably die, and that we will be assailed by all manner of human experiences that cause us to suffer. This is the human condition, and we must wake up to this realisation, learn to embrace, understand, and accept it, and not block it out, ignore, or fight it. This awareness and recognition of the fragility of our lives may help us to take individual responsibility for making choices, for finding meaning, and living authentically, truthfully, and courageously—we only get one chance to live our lives. 'It's not a dress rehearsal,' as the saying goes! Rather than live our lives based on our social identities, we may begin to look behind, beneath, or beyond these, to find our true selves and a deeper meaning to our lives by beginning to create and live by our own maps, rather than those of others, or those created for us like our social identities.

8.   Mindfulness and living beyond the ego:

Learn to live in the moment through practising mindfulness. Just observe your moment-to-moment experience, your thoughts, feelings, and sensations as these arise, and accept them freely, with equanimity and curiosity, but without judgement or secondary appraisal (i.e. do not react to these). In order to learn to live in the present and self-regulate your attention, cultivate your capacities for non-distraction, letting go, non-elaboration of thoughts, and attention switching. In this way you may be able to separate (and decentre) yourself from your negative internal dialogues, states, and perspectives as these arise and see these as just that and not as real; and, therefore, as things that define, reflect, or determine your sense of self.

Realise that much of your suffering is related to your satisfying the needs of your ego and senses; to your attachment to material objects in the world; to your dualistic thinking (e.g. good-bad, happy-sad, fair-unfair, success-failure, winner-loser); to your self-interest, greed, anger, avarice, power, jealousy, fear; to your belief (or illusion) that you have control over events. Learn to stand back and think about the motives for, and origins of, your actions, thoughts, and feelings.

9.   The self in relation to the social world:

In your everyday living, you necessarily inhabit a never-ending multitude of socially, linguistically, discursively, institutionally, and culturally constructed selves, identities, personhoods, narratives, and subject positions, each with their prescribed behaviours. It follows, therefore, that you have the power to change and re-define these for yourself, from those that are negative to those that are more positive for your psychological well-being.

For example, in your suffering, you do not have to be, inhabit, act-out, or have a life-narrative of a person who is depressed, anxious, or a victim, failure, loser, the dumped person, a loner, unlovable, stupid, fat, ugly, mad, the criminal, deviant, the addict, the alcoholic, bereaved or disabled.

You can, instead, take on or develop more positive constructs, positions, and narratives for yourself e.g. survivor, strong, confident, wise, intelligent, talented, stable, valued, a good worker, kind, optimistic, happy and contented, or a glass half-full person, and someone who enjoys their own company, and is socially popular. In doing this, your thoughts, attitudes, beliefs, feelings, and behaviours may change accordingly and reduce your emotional and psychological distress and suffering.

10. Living in the real world:

Reality is constituted in real objects and structures in the world which have deep, intrinsic, underlying and enduring properties, and contingent (or necessary) relationships, which have capacity and power to act in certain ways by virtue of these properties, such as tutor-student (the power to give good grades); landlord-tenant (the power to evict); employer-employee (the power to sack); husband-wife (the power to divorce); doctor-patient (the power to save life); state-citizen (the power to confer legal rights); capital-labour (the power to create employment and control wages); judge-criminal (the power to imprison); general-soldier (the power to order into battle, with possible loss of life); benefits agency-claimant (the power to withdraw financial support).

Therefore, despite being able to control your thoughts, feelings and behaviours, the real external world and the necessary and contingent relationships you have in it can, and do, still impact on you materially. Therefore, you need to be able, when necessary, to change this external world socioeconomically, culturally, legally, and politically (e.g. personal relationships, employment, income, housing, health, education, political activity, and representation). Whilst doing this takes personal power to achieve, it also increases personal empowerment.

Bibliography

Aggs, C., Bambling, M., 'Teaching mindfulness to psychotherapists in clinical practice: the mindful therapy programme', *Counselling and Psychotherapy Research*, 10/4 (2010), 278-286.

Bhasker, R., *The Possibility of Naturalism: A Philosophical Critique of the Contemporary Human Sciences*, Brighton: Harvester Press (1979), in Smith, M. J., *Social Science in Question*, London: Sage Publications/The Open University (1998).

Bhasker, R., *Scientific Realism and Human Emancipation*, London: Verso (1986), in Smith, M.J., *Social Science in Question*, London: Sage Publications/The Open University (1998).

Bhasker, R., *Philosophy and the Idea of Freedom*, Oxford: Blackwell (1991), in Smith, M. J., *Social Science in Question*, London: Sage Publications/The Open University (1998).

Bishop, S.R., Lau, M., Shapiro, S., Carlson, L., Anderson, N.D., Carmody, J., et al., 'Mindfulness: A proposed operational definition', *Clinical Psychology: Science and Practice*, 11 (2004), 230-241, in Aggs, C. & Bambling, M. (2010).

Blake, W., *Collected Works (ed.cit.)*, (1927), 108, in Wilson, C., *The Outsider*, London: Picador (1978), 251.

Charlton, B., *Psychiatry and the Human Condition*, Oxford: Radcliffe Medical Press (2000).

Christopher, J.C., Maris, J.A., 'Integrating mindfulness as self-care into counselling and psychotherapy training', *Counselling and Psychotherapy Research*, 10/2 (2010), 114-125.

Cleary, T., (Trans. & Ed.) *Zen Essence: The Science of Freedom*, Boston & London: Shambhala (1995).

Cosmides, L., 'Better than Rational: Evolutionary Psychology and the Invisible Hand', *The American Economic Review*, 82/2, (May 1994), 327-328.

Dalai Lama, *His Holiness the Dalai Lama: My Spiritual Autobiography*, New York: Rider (2011).

Damasio, A., *The Feeling of What Happens: body, emotion and the making of consciousness*, London: Vintage (1999).

Dawkins, R., *The Selfish Gene*, New York City: Oxford University Press (1976).

Dawkins, R., 'Darwin's Dangerous Disciple, An interview by Frank Miele', *Skeptic* magazine, 3/4 (1995).

du Gay, P., Evans, J., Redman, P. (eds.), *'Identity: A Reader'*, London: Sage Publications/The Open University (2000).

du Gay, P., 'Marcel Mauss: Techniques of the body and categories of the person', *Study Guide Block 3, D853, 'Identity in Question'*, The Open University (2000), 26.

Elliot, T.S., 'The Hollow Men' (1925), in Wilson, C., (1978) *The Outsider*, London: Picador (1978), 166.

Eysenck, H., *Dimensions of Personality*, London: Routledge (1947).

Gross, R.D., *Psychology: The Science of Mind and Behaviour*, London: Hodder & Stoughton (1993).

Gurdjieff, G., in Ouspensky, P.D., *In Search of the Miraculous*, Routledge & Kegan, Paul (1950), in Wilson, C.,(1978), 282-283.

Heppner, W.L., Kernis, M.H., Lakey, C.E., Campbell, W.K., Goldman, B.M., Davis, P.J., & Casio, E.V., 'Mindfulness as a means of reducing aggressive behaviour: Dispositional and situational evidence', *Aggressive Behaviour* (2008), 34, 486-496.

Hesse, H., *Steppenwolf* (1929), in Wilson, C., *The Outsider*, London: Picador (1978), 251.

Hodgins, H.S., & Knee, C.R., *'The integrating self and conscious experience'*, in Deci, E. L. & Ryan, R. M. (Eds.), *Handbook of self-determination research*, New York: University of Rochester Press (2002), 87-100.

Jung, C., *The Archetypes and the Collective Unconscious* London (1996).

Jung, C., *Psychological Types*, Zurich: Rascher Verlag (1921).

Kabat-Zinn, J., Introduction, in Fabrizio, D. (Ed.), *Clinical handbook of mindfulness*, New York: Springer (2009), xxv-xxxxiii, in Aggs, C. & Bambling, M. (2010).

Kelly, T.M., 'Thought recognition and psychological well-being: An empirical test of principle based correctional counselling', *Counselling and Psychotherapy Research*, 11/2 (June 2011), 140-147.

Klein, J., *Our Need for Others and its Roots in Infancy*, London: Routledge (1997).

Mauss, M., 'A Category of the human mind: the notion of person; the notion of self' (1938), Chapter 26, in du Gay, et al. (eds.) (2000).

McFarquhar, H., 'Legal Personality', *Offprints, D853, Identity in Question*, The Open University (2000), 193-198.

Millman, D., *Way of the Peaceful Warrior*, California: H. J Kramer and New World Library (2000).

Parlett, M. & Page, F., Gestalt therapy, in Dryden, W. (ed.), *Individual Therapy: A Handbook*, Open University Press (1990), 175-198.

Pinker, S., *How the Mind Works*, W. W. Norton & Company (1997).

Prabhupada, A.C.B.S., *Bhagavad Gita As It Is*, New York, Los Angeles, London and Bombay: The Bhaktivedanta Book Trust (1972).

Pransky, G., *The renaissance of psychology*. New York: Sulzburger & Graham Publishing (1997).

Ransom, J., *Self-realisation through Yoga and Mysticism*, London: The Theosophical Publishing House (1936).

Redman, P., 'The Subject of Language: The Theorisation of Identity in Cultural Studies', *Study Guide Block 1, D853, Identity in Question*, The Open University (2000).

Rogers, C., *Client-centered Therapy: Its Current Practice, Implications and Theory*. London: Constable (1951).

Rogers, C., 'A Theory of Therapy, Personality and Interpersonal Relationships as Developed in the Client-centered Framework', in (ed.) Koch, S., *Psychology: A Study of a Science. Vol. 3: Formulations of the Person and the Social Context*. New York: McGraw Hill (1959).

Segal, Z.V., Williams, J.M., & Teasdale, J.D., '*Mindfulness-based cognitive therapy for depression: A new approach to preventing relapse*', New York: The Guildford Press (2002), in Aggs, C. & Bambling, M. (2010).

Shakespeare, W., *Hamlet*, New Haven and London: Yale University Press (2003).

Shakespeare, W., *Romeo and Juliet*, New Haven and London: Yale University Press (2004).

Shakespeare, W., *Othello*, London: Penguin (2005).

Shakespeare, W., *Macbeth*, Oxford and New York: Oxford University Press (2008).

Shapiro, S.L., & Carlson, L.E., Astin, J.A., & Freedman, B., 'Mechanisms of mindfulness', *Journal of Clinical Psychology*, 62 (2006), 373-386, in Aggs, C. & Bambling, M. (2010).

Smith, M. J, *Social Science in Question*, London: Sage Publications/ The Open University (1998).

Thorne, B., 'A Collision of Worlds', *Therapy Today*, 20/4 (2009), 22-25.

Weber, M., *The Protestant Ethic and the Spirit of Capitalism* (1904 and 1905).

Wilber, K., *No Boundary: Eastern and Western Approaches to Personal Growth*, Boston: Shambhala (1985).

Wilson, C., *The Outsider*, London: Picador (1978).

Wilson, P., *The Calm Technique: Simple meditation methods that really work*, Northamptonshire: Thorsons Publishers Limited (1987).

Appendix A

The Human Condition: A Schematic Representation of its Levels, Components, and Processes

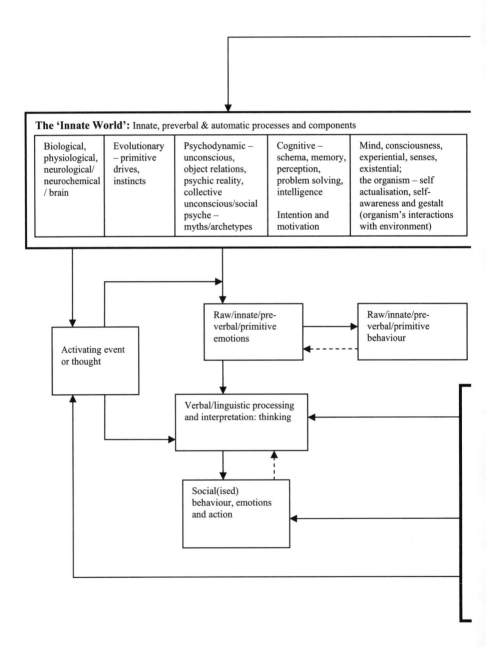

The 'Innate World': Innate, preverbal & automatic processes and components

| Biological, physiological, neurological/ neurochemical / brain | Evolutionary – primitive drives, instincts | Psychodynamic – unconscious, object relations, psychic reality, collective unconscious/social psyche – myths/archetypes | Cognitive – schema, memory, perception, problem solving, intelligence

Intention and motivation | Mind, consciousness, experiential, senses, existential; the organism – self actualisation, self-awareness and gestalt (organism's interactions with environment) |

Raw/innate/pre-verbal/primitive emotions

Raw/innate/pre-verbal/primitive behaviour

Activating event or thought

Verbal/linguistic processing and interpretation: thinking

Social(ised) behaviour, emotions and action

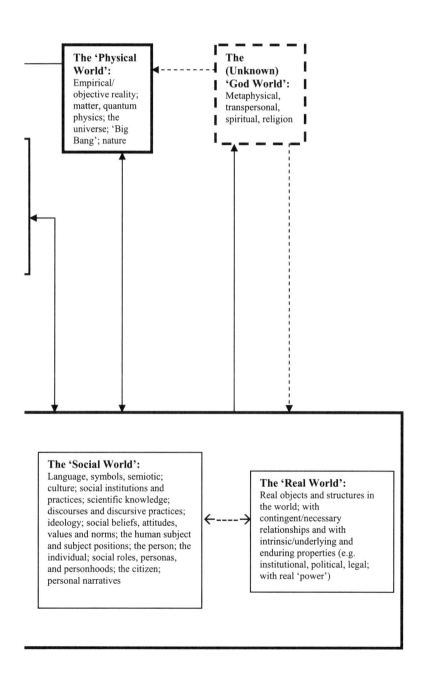